CW01429921

New-Dialect Formation

For Derry and Elizabeth
and all the other human, canine and feline Gordons

New-Dialect Formation
the inevitability of colonial Englishes

Peter Trudgill

Edinburgh University Press

© Peter Trudgill, 2004, 2006

Edinburgh University Press Ltd
22 George Square, Edinburgh

Typeset in Ehrhardt
by Koinonia, Manchester, and
printed and bound in Great Britain by
MPG Books Ltd, Bodmin, Cornwall

First published in hardback by
Edinburgh University Press in 2004

A CIP record for this book is available from the British Library

ISBN 0 7486 1877 5 (paperback)

The right of Peter Trudgill
to be identified as author of this work
has been asserted in accordance with
the Copyright, Designs and Patents Act 1988.

Contents

Preface

For the past several Northern Hemisphere winters I have been fortunate enough to have been invited to work as a consultant for the Origins of New Zealand English (ONZE) Project, led by Professor Elizabeth Gordon, in the Linguistics Department at the University of Canterbury, Christchurch, New Zealand. This project is without any doubt the most exciting academic project I have had the good fortune to be associated with. It owes most of all to Elizabeth Gordon's vision, insight and energy, and its results have an importance way beyond the shores of New Zealand. I am very grateful to her for allowing me to work on the uniquely rich data source on which the project is based. I am also very grateful indeed to the other colleagues on the project, especially my co-authors on a number of papers (in addition to Elizabeth Gordon), Margaret Maclagan and Gillian Lewis, as well as to Lyle Campbell. Invaluable support of various types was also provided at different times by Mike Clayton, Leigh Nurkka and Stacey Nicholas. Although not all of my ONZE Project colleagues will agree with all of the conclusions presented in this book, I could not have arrived at these conclusions without them. The results of the research of the ONZE Project to date are to be found in a number of papers, by the various project members named here, which are listed in the references. The most important work to stem from the project, however, is the Cambridge University Press book by Elizabeth Gordon et al., *New Zealand English: its origins and evolution* (2004). Some of the phonological material presented in Chapter 2 of the present book can also be found there.

It will be clear from my text that I owe an enormous debt to the work of John Wells, whose seminal book, *English Accents*, is cited here many, many times. And I am also very grateful to the following, who have read and commented on earlier versions of this text and of previous work from which it is derived: Enam Al-Wer, Laurie Bauer, Allan Bell, Raphael Berthele, David Britain, Magdalena Charzynska-Wójcik, Helen Christen, Mercedes Durham, Derry Gordon, Walter Haas, Jean Hannah, Janet Holmes, Paul Kerswill, Klaus Mattheier, Daniel Schreier and Jürg Schwyter. It goes without saying that none of the deficiencies in this volume are their responsibility, but I am going to say it anyway.

THE DATABASE

The New Zealand English evidence I use in this book comes from the remarkable data archive just referred to. This consists of recordings made for the National Broadcasting Corporation of New Zealand between 1946 and 1948 by their Mobile Disc Recording Unit, which travelled around small towns in both the North Island and South Island of New Zealand. The recordings were of pioneer reminiscences, mostly from people who were children of the first European settlers in New Zealand. About 325 speakers born between 1850 and 1900 were recorded before the enterprise was brought to a premature end in 1948. In 1989, Elizabeth Gordon arranged to purchase copies of all these recordings, which now form the basis of the Origins of New Zealand English (ONZE) Project at the Department of Linguistics at Christchurch. These have subsequently been re-recorded, digitalised, catalogued, transcribed, and supplemented by genealogical information about the speakers obtained from archival research and from contacts with the speakers' relatives and descendants, as well as from local historical research concerning settlement patterns in the areas in question.

The New Zealand data in what follows is derived from this ONZE Mobile Unit Corpus, and is based on analyses I was fortunate enough to have been permitted to make of recordings of eighty-four speakers from thirty-four different locations in New Zealand, both North Island and South Island, who were born between 1850 and 1889, which I take to be the crucial formation period for New Zealand English (see below). The eighty-four speakers are both male and female and come from a whole range of walks of life: this is the nearest thing possible to a representative sample of the native anglophone New Zealand population born between these two dates. Fascinatingly, none of these speakers sound like modern New Zealanders; some of them sound like English or Scottish or Irish people; and many of them sound like no one at all except themselves ...

Data concerning Australian English in what follows have been taken from published sources cited in the text, as well as from notes made during my three-month-long visit to Australia in 1982. South African English data are based for the most part on published sources, but also on my observations over the years of the speech of South African English speakers, live, and in the broadcast media. Data on Falkland Islands English are taken from Sudbury's pioneering thesis (2000), as well as from my recordings, notes and analyses of speakers of Falkland Islands English as they appeared very frequently on British radio and TV during and after the Falklands conflict, as well as from analyses made of the 2003 BBC Radio 4 programme series *Falkland Families*. Data on the English of Tristan da Cunha are taken from Dani Schreier's equally pioneering work (Schreier, 2003), as well as from my own analyses of recordings made by Schreier on Tristan and kindly made available by him, and especially (because older) of recordings made of Tristanians, when they were in England in the 1961, and kindly made available to me by *The Survey of English Usage* at University College, London University.

In what follows I argue for the most part, although not entirely, from the linguistic data. I look at the linguistic facts as these have been presented to me on the tapes in the ONZE Mobile Unit archive and the other sources. I also look at linguistic data concerning what is known about the nineteenth-century English of the British Isles which gave rise to the Southern Hemisphere Englishes. (In my discussion I will often for simplicity use the adjective 'British' to relate to the country that was in the nineteenth century officially 'The United Kingdom of Britain and Ireland'. I will also, however, use the term 'British Isles' to indicate that I am talking about the two separate islands of Ireland and Britain, even though Irish friends have indicated that Irish people do not necessarily approve of this term either.) There will also be references in the book to data from other colonial varieties of English, and other languages. However, I do not examine in any detail migration demographics, studies of settlement patterns, sociological analyses, or economic facts, though of course such studies have their place. I do use geodemographic information at crucial points in what follows, but I have preferred wherever possible to agree with McWhorter (2000: 165) when he says, of similar historical reconstruction work on creole language origins: 'Many creolists tend to see the socio-historical evidence as decisive, and as a welcome improvement upon linguistic evidence considered merely tangential, capable only of "suggestion". In fact, one can argue that things are precisely the other way around.' I will attempt for the most part to let the linguistic facts speak for themselves.

Maps

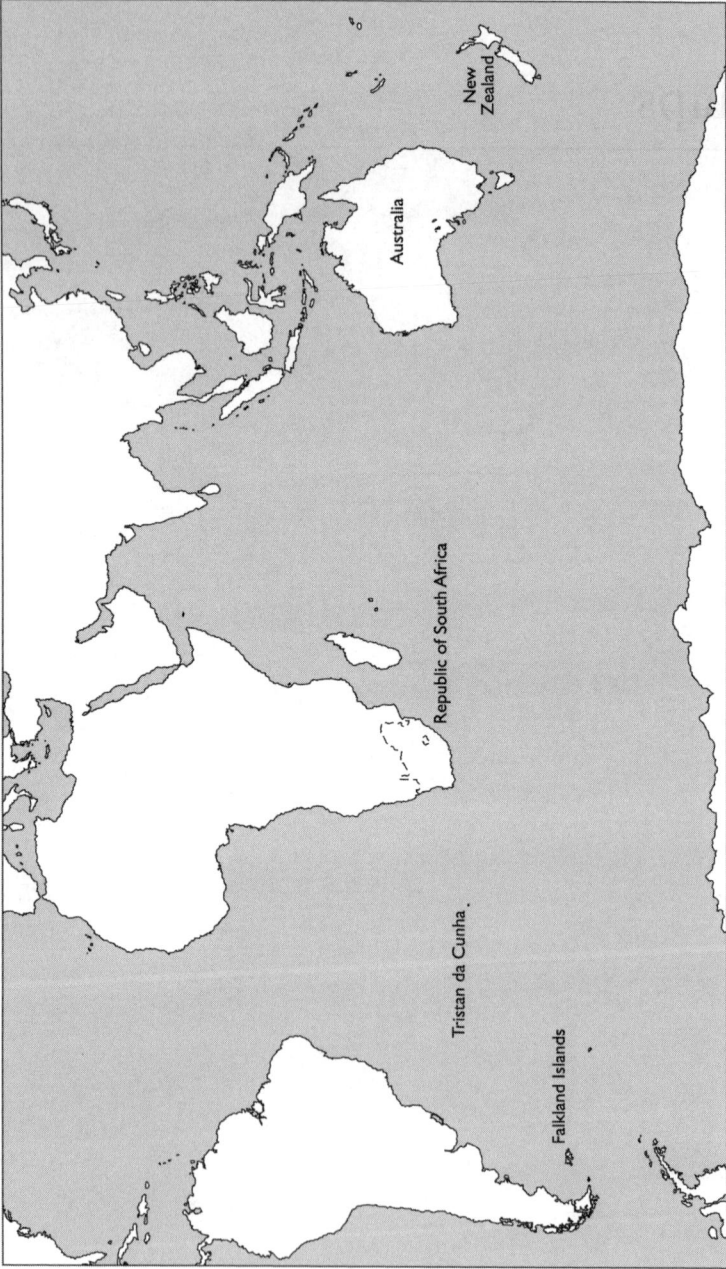

I Southern Hemisphere

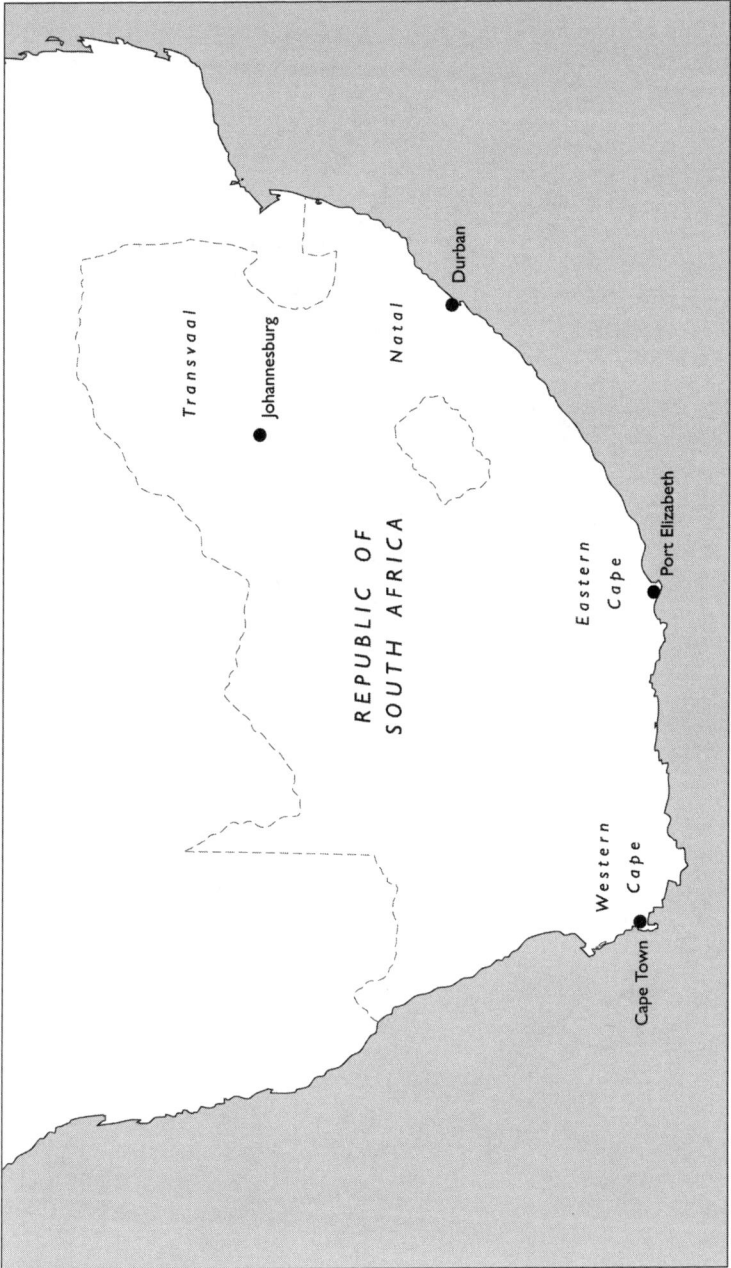

II Republic of South Africa

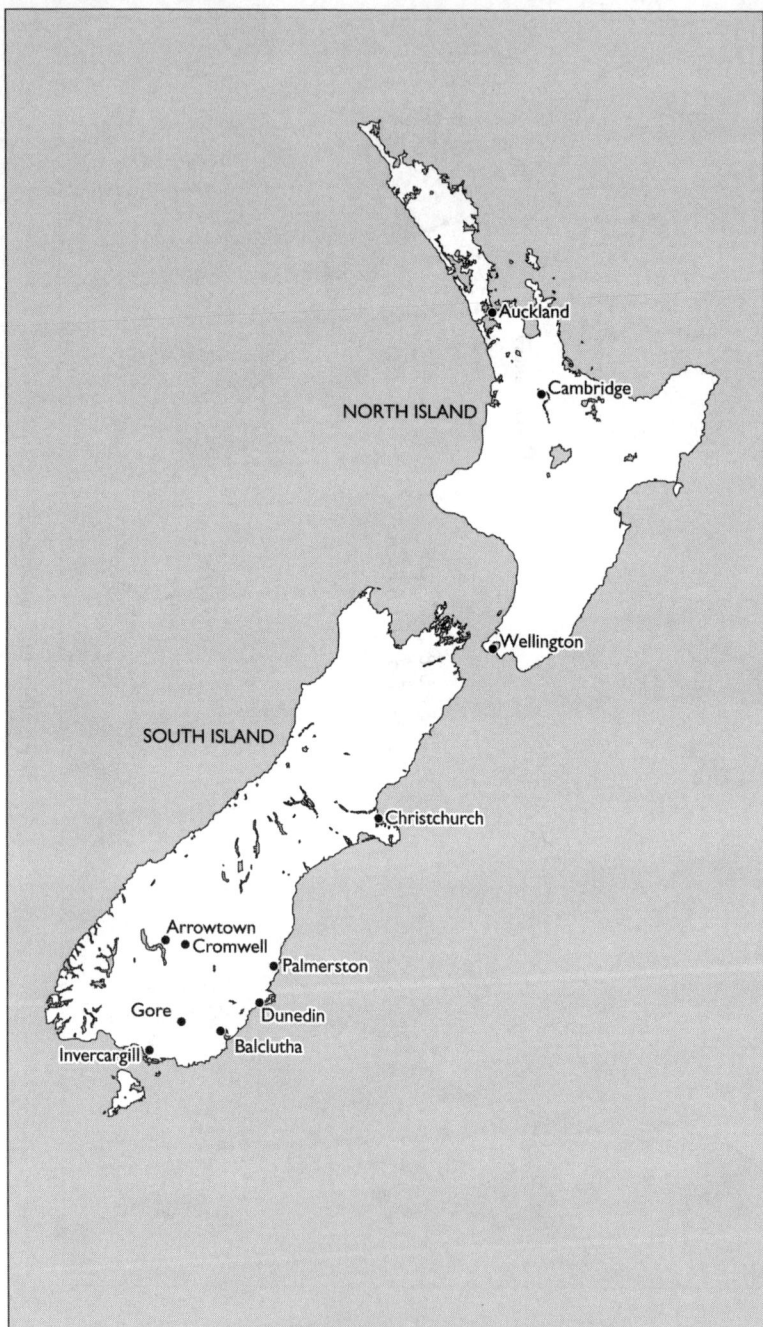

III New Zealand

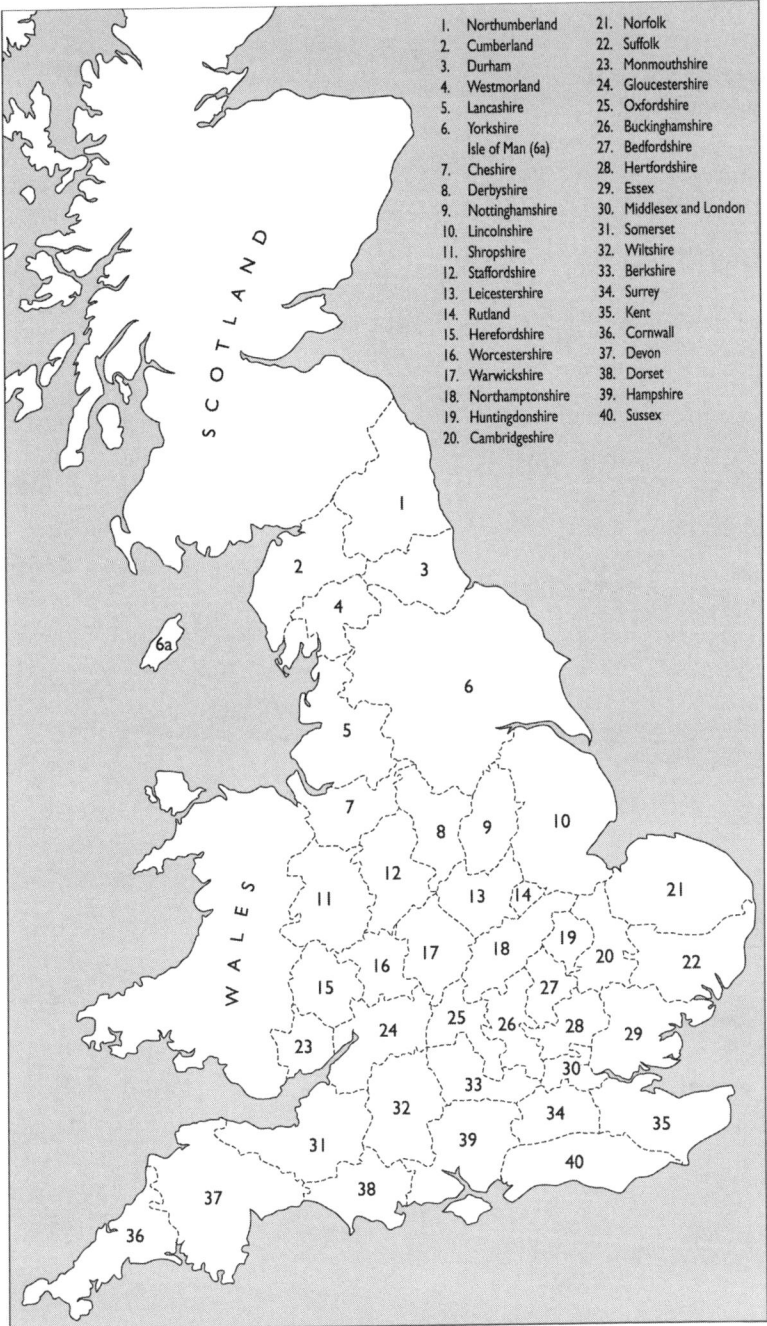

1.	Northumberland	21.	Norfolk
2.	Cumberland	22.	Suffolk
3.	Durham	23.	Monmouthshire
4.	Westmorland	24.	Gloucestershire
5.	Lancashire	25.	Oxfordshire
6.	Yorkshire	26.	Buckinghamshire
	Isle of Man (6a)	27.	Bedfordshire
7.	Cheshire	28.	Hertfordshire
8.	Derbyshire	29.	Essex
9.	Nottinghamshire	30.	Middlesex and London
10.	Lincolnshire	31.	Somerset
11.	Shropshire	32.	Wiltshire
12.	Staffordshire	33.	Berkshire
13.	Leicestershire	34.	Surrey
14.	Rutland	35.	Kent
15.	Herefordshire	36.	Cornwall
16.	Worcestershire	37.	Devon
17.	Warwickshire	38.	Dorset
18.	Northamptonshire	39.	Hampshire
19.	Huntingdonshire	40.	Sussex
20.	Cambridgeshire		

IV United Kingdom showing the old English counties

Vowel Charts

Unrounded

Rounded

CHAPTER 1

Colonial dialects as mixed dialects

If we attempt to explain why colonial Englishes – for example American English – are different from the English of Britain, whence they originally came, it is reasonably clear what explanatory factors should be proposed:

1. American English (for instance) has adapted to new topographical and biological features unknown in Britain: for example, as is well known, the word *robin* in North America refers to a bird which is different from its referent in Britain; and the word *bluff* has been extended to refer to a cliff or headland along a river.

2. Since the departure of English for America, linguistic changes have occurred in Britain which have not occurred in North America: for example, the glottalling of intervocalic and word-final /t/, as in *better, bet*, is typical of British but not of North American English (Wells, 1982).

3. Since the arrival of English from Britain, linguistic changes have taken place in America which have not occurred in Britain: for example, the voicing of intervocalic /t/ and the flapping of intervocalic /t/ and /d/ as in *city, ready* are typical of North American and not of British English (Wells, 1982).

4. American English has experienced forms of language contact with indigenous languages which have, obviously, not been experienced by British English: for example, American English has borrowed lexical items such as *skunk* and *caucus* from Native American languages (Romaine, 2001).

5. American English has experienced forms of language contact with other European languages in the colonial situation (Romaine, 2001) which have not been experienced by British English: for example, American English has borrowed lexical items such as *cookie* 'biscuit' from Dutch and *key* 'islet' from Spanish. We can also suppose that North American grammatical constructions such as *Are you coming with?* and *I like to skate* (as opposed to *I like skating)* are the result of German and/or Yiddish influence (see Trudgill, 1986a; Mufwene, 2001: 162).

There is also, however, one other important factor which has to be taken into consideration.

6. From the very beginning, American English was subject to processes associated with *dialect contact*. Although of course the geographical and social origins of the settlers were different in each location, none of the early anglophone settlements on the east coast of what is now the United States was settled from a single location in England. We can therefore assume that, very early on, contact between different British dialects would have occurred in the American settlements, which would have led to the appearance of new, mixed dialects not precisely like any dialect spoken in the homeland. These were all, as Kurath has said, 'a unique blend of British types of speech' (1949: 1). The fact of modern regional variation along the east coast of the USA is thus explained not only in terms of different linguistic changes having taken place in different areas during the last 400 years, but also more crucially by the fact that the initial mixtures – and, therefore, the outcomes of these mixtures – were different in the different places from the very beginning (see Algeo, 2001). In the words of McDavid (1985: 19), we can assume 'dialect mixture from the beginning in each colony ... with different results'.

In most cases, the mixture processes which gave rise to the original East Coast varieties of American English are hard to detect because the processes took place more than 300 years ago, although in some cases traces of origins and of mixing may still be visible. For instance, Eastern New England English still preserves the East Anglian short o (Trudgill, 2002) in items like *boat*; but on the other hand it also has the THOUGHT–LOT Merger (note that in this book I use the keywords for lexical sets established by Wells, 1982), the only origin of which in Britain could have been Scotland. Southern dialects of American English have double modals, as in *I might could go*, which have a northern origin in England, and yet they have the southern England FOOT–STRUT Split. Midland dialects show clear northern Irish influence (Montgomery, 1998); for example, they have *ways* rather than *way*, as in *it's a long ways to go*; and yet they do not have other northern Irish features such as the partial THOUGHT–LOT Merger.

Similarities between the metropolitan and colonial varieties can of course be due (mostly) to shared retentions, but can also be due (unusually) to shared innovations, an issue we shall discuss later.

COLONIAL ENGLISHES

It seems likely that, just as in the case of American English, the linguistic characteristics of nearly all other colonial varieties of English, and of other languages, are also the result of a combination of factors 1–6.

Factor 1, adaptation to a new physical environment, seems to be a general phenomenon. For Canadian French, for example, Mougeon and Beniak (1994: 26) discuss 'French neologisms which referred to concepts or realities typical of the New World'. It also seems to be a phenomenon which does not differ greatly in importance as between one form of colonial English and another, although it is possible that, say, the topography of New Zealand posed fewer nomenclature problems for people from Britain than that of Australia.

Factors 2 and 3, different linguistic changes in the mother country and the colony, will obviously, other things being equal, increase in importance as time goes by. We would therefore expect these factors to play a bigger role in the differentiation of, say, Bahamian English from British English than in the case of the Falkland Islands, given that the settlement of the Bahamas by English speakers began in 1648 while that of the Falklands began only in 1841, at the very earliest.

The importance of factor 4, language contact with indigenous languages, will depend on who, if anybody, was in the new location before the anglophone settlers arrived. We would not expect to find any influence of indigenous language contact in Bermudan or Falkland Islands or Tristan da Cunha English for the obvious reason that these islands had never had an indigenous population prior to the arrival of anglophone settlers. On the other hand, we can look for influence from Native American languages in Canada and the United States, Maori in New Zealand, Australian languages in Australia, and Bantu and Khoisan in South Africa.

Contact with indigenous languages seems to manifest itself mostly in terms of the acquisition of loanwords from these languages. South African English has forms such as *karroo* 'desert plateau' and *dagga* 'wild hemp' from Khoi, and *bundu* 'rough country' and *impala* 'type of antelope' from Bantu languages (Branford, 1994). Australia had perhaps 200 aboriginal languages at the time of first European settlement (Dixon, 1980), but they have had no influence on mainstream Australian English other than the loaning of a number of words, most often for indigenous flora and fauna and placenames, including well-known items such as *kangaroo* (from Guugu Yimidhirr) and *boomerang* (from Dharuk). Australia also has an English-based creole known as Kriol, or Bamyili Creole, spoken natively by about 10,000 aboriginal people in northern areas of Western Australia, Northern Territory, and Queensland, and by even more second-language speakers, but this has had no effect on mainstream Australian English as such.

The Eastern Polynesian language Maori had already been in New Zealand for 650–800 years at the time of European colonisation; there were perhaps 200,000 Maori at this period (Sinclair, 1959), and there were many Europeans – including, as they make clear in their stories, some of the Mobile Unit informants – who became less or more fluent in Maori. We do have reports of a Maori–English pre-pidgin from the nineteenth century, though nothing of this has survived (Clark, 1990). It is true, too, that considerable numbers of Maori words are now current in and known by most speakers of New Zealand English though, with a very few exceptions such as *mana* 'honour, prestige, authority, status, charisma', they are mostly employed in connection with indigenous flora and fauna and with Maori cultural practices only. Recent work has also suggested that there is now a distinctively Maori form of the New Zealand English accent, though its history remains obscure (Holmes, 1997; Bell and

Kuiper, 2000). However, it is clear that language contact between Maori and English has in the long run had a greater effect on the former than on the latter.

The importance of factor 5, language contact with other European languages, will also depend on circumstances. We would not expect to find any influence of such contact at all in early Bermudan English, given that the settlers all came from England. On the other hand, American English, as we saw, does demonstrate a number of results of contact with other European languages. South African English shows many signs of contact with Afrikaans. Falkland Islands English has some words from Spanish. Tristan da Cunha English, because of its settlement history (see Schreier, 2003), shows a number of very clear signs of language contact. Cape Breton Island English, Nova Scotia, shows considerable influence from Scottish Gaelic. And the colonial English of the *Confederados* of Americana, Brazil (Montgomery and Melo, 1990), has had very considerable contact with Portuguese.

In some cases, the relative influence of factors 4 and 5 as opposed to 6 – language contact versus dialect contact – may be rather hard to disentangle. African American Vernacular English (AAVE), for example, is clearly the result of a complex mixture process. McWhorter (2000), following the arguments outlined by Hancock in many persuasive publications (see, for example, Hancock, 1986), has convincingly suggested that the very many similarities between the Atlantic English Creoles can be explained in terms of them all having descended from a single English–lexifier pidgin that developed in West Africa (specifically, according to McWhorter, at Cormantin, Ghana) in the 1600s. This was subsequently transported to the Western Hemisphere, where it was creolised just once, in Barbados (or, possibly, St Kitts), whence it was transported further to many other locations in the Americas. In South Carolina, this creole acted as 'one of the sources of African-American Vernacular English' (McWhorter, 2000: 240), the other inputs being dialects of English. (In other words, those scholars favouring an exclusively British Isles or an exclusively African and/or creole origin for AAVE are both wrong.)

The English of Tristan da Cunha also has a very complex contact history. It has a number of different dialect features from different parts of the British Isles and the USA, but it also has a number of features which are clearly due to language contact. It is probably, for instance, the only variety of native-speaker English to use 'double past tense marking' or 'past tense infinitive' constructions, as in *he didn't want to went*. Since this is normally a feature only of foreign learners' English, it makes sense to ascribe it to language contact. As Schreier (2003) points out, this could be contact, in this very small community, with a small number of speakers of European languages – Danish, Dutch, Italian – and/or with a possibly creoloid English-lexifier variety from St Helena – in which case this was language contact with a variety which was itself already the result of language contact. For the relative importance of the roles of language and dialect contact in the genesis of Tristan da Cunha phonology, see Schreier and Trudgill (forthcoming).

Similarly, Caribbean forms of English show influence of descent from the original Atlantic English Creole, but are also often said to show input from different regional Englishes, such as that of Ireland (Rickford, 1986).

Similar issues are bound to occur in studying the origins of other colonial varieties. For example, Lipski (1994) points out that, in considering why Latin American Spanish is as it is, it is necessary not only to look at the input from Iberian Spanish but also to consider the role of the indigenous languages such as Quechua (pp. 62–92); the influence of African languages (pp. 93–135); and of other languages, notably Italian especially in the case of the Spanish of Buenos Aires and Montevideo (167, 175–9). Penny (2000: 147) discusses the retention of Spanish /ʎ/ (as opposed to change to /j/) in those areas of South America where the indigenous languages such as Quechua also have /ʎ/. Mattoso Camara (1972: 20) discusses the input to Brazilian Portuguese from African languages such as Yoruba, as well as indigenous languages such as Tupi. And Darot and Pauleau discuss the role of local Austronesian languages, together with Australian English, in the development of the French of New Caledonia (Darot and Pauleau, 1993).

There is also a big issue in the study of the development of Canadian French which has to do with the extent to which the original colonisers actually spoke 'French' or not (see Asselin and McLaughlin, 1994). Many francophone linguists discussing this issue distinguish between French, including standard and regional varieties of French, on the one hand, and *patois*, on the other

(Barbaud, 1994). Here, *patois* would appear to be equivalent to Wells's (1982) term 'Traditional-dialect', but the implications of these discussions is that the structural differences between the patois, and between the patois and French, were sufficiently great for us to be able to consider that there was a kind of language contact that took place in Canada, in addition to the dialect contact which obviously also occurred. This is so even though only between 4% and 8% of the colonists came from the southern *langue d'oc* area and could therefore have been uncontroversially described as being speakers of a language other than French (i.e. Provençal/Occitan).

DIALECT CONTACT AND COLONIAL DIALECTS

The importance of factor 6, dialect contact, will also vary. The vast majority of colonial Englishes do show the results of such contact, but I acknowledge some exceptions. These are cases where settlements were derived from single locations and no mixing could occur. For example, rural dialects of Newfoundland English (i.e. not that of the dialect of the capital, St John's) are derived more or less directly either from the English southwest or the Irish southeast (Paddock, 1982; Kirwin, 2001). Rural Falkland Islands English (i.e. not the dialect of the capital, Port Stanley) also differs from settlement to settlement depending on the origins of each community in a single British location (Sudbury, 2000; Trudgill, 1986), particularly on West Falkland. My own fieldwork on the English of Cape Breton, Nova Scotia, reveals a variety that is more or less identical with the English of the Scottish Highlands. And the one linguistic colony of the USA that has been studied, the Brazilian settlement of Americana mentioned above, has an English which is entirely derived from the American southeast.

Monogenetic theories

Some writers have rejected the importance of dialect contact in the development of colonial varieties altogether. Poirier (1994), for example, cites Rivard (1914) as suggesting that Quebec French is due to the dialects of Normandy. Lipski similarly (1994: 36) outlines a theory which developed amongst hispanicists that Latin American

Spanish is in origin basically a form of transported Andalusian Spanish from the Iberian Peninsula. This *andalucista* theory, which was proposed early on by Wagner (1920) amongst others, is ultimately discounted by Lipski, who says (p. 61) that 'the formation of Latin American Spanish cannot be reduced to simple formulas'.

I too discount these theories, as well as the similar theories proposed in connection with colonial Englishes (with the obvious exceptions such as West Falkland mentioned above). I do acknowledge that Australasian English is now typologically very close to the English of the southeast of England. However, I do not agree that 'it is clear that New Zealand English derives from a variety of English spoken in the south-east of England' (Bauer, 1997: 391). Nor do I agree with Hammarström's claim (1980) that Australian English is simply transplanted Cockney. Nor do I accept the same Cockney-origin point argued by Wall (1938) for New Zealand English.

South American Spanish resembles Andalusian Spanish, but is not *identical* with it. Quebec French is rather close to the French of the Île de France, but is not identical with it (Mougeon and Beniak, 1994: 33). Similarly, Australasian English resembles London English, but is not identical with it. The undoubted typological resemblances between it and Australasian English cannot simply be the result of the transplantation of London English to the other side of the world. As I pointed out in Trudgill (1986), if there *was* a single location in Britain from which Australian English was transplanted, it would have to be not London but rural Essex, something which I stress is extremely unlikely! My argument is that rural Essex was the only area of England which in the nineteenth century distinguished the vowels of FOOT and STRUT; which was non-rhotic; which had front rather than back /a:/ as in START; and which had schwa rather than the KIT vowel in the unstressed syllables of *David*, *naked*, etc., all four features being characteristic of Australian English. Since it is ludicrous to suppose that rural Essex did in fact provide the sole model input for a transplanted Australian English, it is safe to assume that this particular combination of features must have arisen as a result of mixture. Bauer (2000: 49) writes of 'Trudgill's suggestion that Essex might be one of the sources of the mixed dialect which provided the New Zealand accent' and has thus somewhat misrepresented me on two counts, although I do indeed say that East Anglia, including Essex, would have been *one* of the regional

British Isles inputs into Australian English; and my argument does indeed work equally well for New Zealand English which has the same combination of four phonological features. I do not accept, either, that New Zealand English arrived as a ready-formed entity transplanted in its entirety from Australia. The most notable exponent of this view is Bauer (1997). He writes that 'the hypothesis that New Zealand English is derived from Australian English is the one which explains most about the linguistic situation in New Zealand' (p. 428). We shall see below that there might well have been adolescent speakers of a newly focussed Australian English by about 1855. We also know that many settlers to New Zealand came either from or, more often, via Australia; Bauer himself says that his second argument in favour of the hypothesis that New Zealand English is derived from Australian English 'is the demographic one' – there was and remains close contact between the two countries (in spite of their being 2,250 kilometres apart at the nearest point). This idea, then, is entirely plausible.

However, as McWhorter (2000: 92) has said of another (creole) variety-creation scenario: 'Plausible though this idea be, the linguistic data tell otherwise'. It is true that Bauer argues that there is in fact linguistic evidence for his point of view. His first argument is the close phonological similarity between New Zealand English and Australian English, which I will supply an alternative explanation for below. His other argument comes from vocabulary: 'the number of words which Australia and New Zealand share – virtually to the exclusion of the rest of the English-speaking world – is astounding if the two varieties have independent origins'. In fact, I am not arguing for *totally* independent origins – it is clear that Australian English, insofar as there was such a thing, supplied some of the input to the New Zealand dialect mixture. But in any case we should be very reluctant to accept arguments from vocabulary. Of course I accept Bauer's data about British regional dialect vocabulary in New Zealand English (see below) – there is ultimately nowhere else but the British regions that these lexical items could originally have come from. I also accept that there seem to be many words and usages in New Zealand English which came from Australian English. However, this may be more apparent than real, since at least some of these appear currently to be distinctively Australasian simply because, having originally come from the

British Isles, they have now been lost there e.g. *cobber* 'friend' and *crib* 'lunch', which are cited by Bauer as evidence for the Australasian connection, are in fact both shown by Orsman (1997) to be of British origin, as are *chiack* 'tease', *chook* 'chick(en)', *tucker* 'food' and *larrikin* 'young ruffian' (see also Eagleson, 1982; Trudgill and Hannah, 2002). These then are not shared innovations but shared retentions – a much weaker source of evidence.

And, in any case, arguments for diffusion by emigration based solely on vocabulary are very weak. British English now has scores of lexical items that until the 1930s were found in American English only (Strang, 1970), and the number of such items continues to mount: in my lifetime British people have stopped *hiring* cars and started *renting* them; they now listen to the *radio* rather than the *wireless*; and have become hopelessly confused about the meaning of the word *billion*. But this is not a sign that British English has its *origins* in American English: 'lexical differences are highly salient, and are readily apparent to all speakers of the varieties concerned without any linguistic training or analysis. They are also (mostly) non-systematic, and susceptible to being learned one at a time' (Trudgill, 1986: 25) and to being readily acquired by adults. So, even if a certain amount of New Zealand English vocabulary came from Australia (though vice versa is also of course a possibility), this does not mean that the core phonological and other linguistic characteristics also did so. (Bauer's one grammatical example – that Australian English and New Zealand English both share the construction *NP didn't use(d) to V* rather than *NP used not to V* does not work at all since this usage is also perfectly normal in England (see Hughes and Trudgill, 1995), and I for example have always used this form myself.)

So I do not accept this particular linguistic evidence. On the contrary, I supply some powerful counter-evidence (which, to be fair, was not available to Bauer) against the monogenetic New-Zealand-English-came-from-Australia hypothesis. This evidence comes from the linguistic data supplied by the Mobile Unit speakers and is very clear: none of these speakers sound much like Australians and most of them sound nothing like them at all. New Zealanders born in the decades immediately after 1840 did not speak Australian English. This does not mean, however, that I totally exclude the possibility of Australian influence: Australian English was a small

but occasionally crucially influential part of the input to the dialect
mixture in early New Zealand – as we shall see later.

Dialect mixture – the consensus

These unsuccessful attempts at monogenetic explanations apart,
there seems to be a general consensus in the literature that the
normal position is that colonial varieties are the consequence, at
least in part, of dialect mixture. Branford (1994: 487) supports a
dialect contact origin for South African English, and shows that the
initial English-speaking immigrants to South Africa came from
London, Ireland, Lancashire, Yorkshire and Scotland. Lass, too,
talks about the Scottish as well as English English input in the
formation of South African English (1997: 206). And Lanham
(1967: 104) writes that South African English is derived from 'at
least 20 regional (geographical) dialects' and says that

> out of a welter of English dialects there grew up in a remarkably
> short space of time a form of English which was not identical
> with any one of them but presented a unique set of dialectal
> features deriving probably from several British dialects.

Cochrane (1989) tends to agree for Australia, and Turner (1994:
278), too, writes that early Australia 'was a situation of "dialects in
contact"'. For New Zealand, Bauer (2000) supplies very strong
lexical evidence in favour of the mixed origins of New Zealand
English. And Schreier (2003) discusses the important role of dialect
contact in the development of Tristan da Cunha.

Indeed, the earliest example of English colonial dialect mixture
involves the development of English itself: Nielsen (1998: 77–9)
ascribes some of the characteristics of early Old English to the fact
that it is the result of a mixture of West Germanic dialects from
continental Europe. He points out that it is because of dialect
mixture that Old English had, initially, more variability (cf. Chapter
4) than the other Germanic languages where no colonial dialect
mixture had been involved. For example, Old English had a large
number of different forms for 'first': *ærest* (cf. Old High German
eristo); *forma* (cf. Old Frisian *forma*); *formesta* (cf. Gothic *frumists*);
and *fyrst* (cf. Old Norse *fyrstr*).

Samuels (1972: 108) makes the same point about late medieval colonial English in Ireland. He says that the available texts show that the English settlers 'must have been predominantly from the West Midlands and South-West England', but the language of the texts 'tallies with the dialect of no single restricted area of England; it consists mainly of an amalgam of selected features from the different dialects of a number of areas'.

The literature on colonial varieties of languages other than English also supports this view. An early proponent of such a view was Frings (1957), who described the eastward colonial expansion of German into formerly Slavic-speaking areas as resulting in a new variety which was the result of a mixture of Dutch, Low German, Central German and Upper German dialect forms. This was later to provide the basis for Standard German, which shows a mixture of forms such as the southern pronominal distinction between accusative and dative forms e.g. *mich* 'me (acc.)' and *mir* '(to) me (dat.)', which is absent from northern German, and the central diminutive *–chen* rather than northern *–kin* or southern *–lein*.

Moag (1977) shows that Fiji Hindi is the result, amongst other things, of a mixing of north Indian varieties. Combrink (1978: 72) suggests that Afrikaans is, in part, the result of 'Germanic dialects in close contact', with most of these dialects – 73% of the immigrants – coming from the dialect areas of North Holland, South Holland and Utrecht. And dialect contact was also clearly important in the development of Canadian French (Morin, 1994). Mougeon and Beniak (1994: 25) say that

> the particular conditions associated with emigration to New France [Canada] and with life in the new colony on the St Lawrence led to a unique mixture ['brassage'] of central French, varieties of regional French and perhaps even of certain *patois* … From this mixture there developed a new form of the French language … a unified, coherent, distinctive Quebec variety [my translation].

They also speak (p. 26) of a 'fusion dialectale'. Poirier (1994: 256) reports that 'philological studies have proved the existence, in the middle of the 17th century, of a *koiné* along the St Lawrence which was strongly influenced by the dialects of different French provinces' (my translation).

Darot and Pauleau (1993: 295) point to the presence in the colonial French of New Caledonia in the South Pacific of forms from southern as well as Parisian French; and Hollyman (1979: 623) also cites the occurrence of features from the north of France as well as from the region of Toulouse.

Lipski (1994: 45) also says of colonial Spanish that 'it would seem that a linguistic alchemy acted on the kaleidoscopic jumble of Peninsula languages and dialects to yield Latin American Spanish'. Mattoso Camara (1972: 20) says of Brazilian Portuguese that 'immigrants from both the north and south of Portugal, seemingly in approximately equal numbers, carried their respective dialects to Brazil'. Quoting da Silva Neto (1950: 10), he also suggests that 'the coming together of such diverse dialects in a single overseas center must have set up conditions leading to a sort of linguistic compromise, a new kind of dialect'.

I therefore suggest that the Southern Hemisphere Englishes, like colonial varieties of the other languages just mentioned, are new and distinctive varieties of the English language which arose as a result of dialect contact, dialect mixture and new-dialect formation. The most important ingredients in the mixture that was to lead to the development of these new forms of English were the dialects and accents of the language brought with them by native speakers of English. In Australia, South Africa, New Zealand and the Falklands, the contact was almost entirely between varieties of English from the British Isles. For New Zealand, immigrants arrived from England, Scotland and Ireland in proportions of roughly 50:27:23. There was very little immigration from Wales. There was also some involvement of Australia. North Americans, on the other hand, though present, constituted no more than 1% of the immigrants to New Zealand between 1840 and 1881 (McKinnon, 1997). In the case of Tristanian English, however, there was significant input from the American English of New England (Schreier, 2003).

SOCIAL DIALECT MIXTURE

Prima facie New Zealand evidence in favour of the dialect contact and mixing hypothesis comes from the fact that the Mobile Unit data show that the speech of the first generation of New-Zealand-born English speakers demonstrates a very wide range of features from very many British dialects.

First, the ONZE Project data show that there was clearly a mix of social dialect features in early New Zealand. We can infer from this that a similar situation would have obtained in the other anglophone colonies. There is today in New Zealand English a social continuum of accents, with the 'broader' accents of the bottom of the social scale being the most distinctively New Zealand (i.e. having more features which are more different from RP). This corresponds to, and no doubt is also at least in part a consequence of, the fact that there is a wide range of social accents in the ONZE archive, although there are no RP speakers as such. All of the ONZE speakers, that is, have features which can be traced back to regional accents in the British Isles. Many speakers use clearly lower-class, stigmatised features such as H Dropping and the pronunciation of *anything*, *something* with final /k/.

The grammatical input into modern New Zealand English was also very mixed, both socially and regionally, according to evidence from the ONZE archive. From the perspective of social dialects, we can note that about 50% of the ONZE speakers demonstrate at least some nonstandard grammatical features. These include the following:

1. There is a strong tendency in nonstandard varieties of English around the world for irregular verbs to have become less irregular, either by total regularisation, as in *know, knowed, knowed*, or by the reduction of three different verb forms for the present, preterite and past participle, as in *write, wrote, written*, to two, as in *write, writ, writ*, just like for regular verbs as in *love, loved, loved*. On the ONZE recordings, preterite *seen* is especially common, as in:

   I seen him go in.

   For some verbs, one form may even be found throughout the

paradigm, as in *come, come, come*. In our archive, preterite *come* is as usual as *came*:

He come home the next night.

2. Nearly all nonstandard dialects of English around the world differ from Standard English in having different morphologies for main verb as opposed to auxiliary verb *do*. Thus the preterite of the auxiliary verb is *did*, as in Standard English, but the preterite of the main verb is *done*. Very many of the ONZE informants demonstrate this pattern, and produce forms such as

We often done that, didn't we?

3. The verb *to be* is irregular in various ways in all varieties of English, but many nonstandard dialects show a certain amount of regularisation. On the ONZE tapes there are some instances of this. Some informants have generalised *were* to all persons, for example:

There were a mill in town.

Others have carried out the reverse process and generalised *was* to the plural also:

The Maoris was there.

4. Most nonstandard dialects of English have multiple negation, and many of the ONZE informants have this also:

We couldn't get none.

5. Many nonstandard dialects of English in Britain and elsewhere have demonstrative reinforcement in which *this here* and *that there* are more common than simple *this* and *that*. ONZE informants also show this usage:

This here place.

REGIONAL DIALECT MIXTURE

Second, there is also in the ONZE Project archive a clear mix of British Isles regional dialect features. Again, this must have been true of the other, earlier colonies. As we saw above, in terms of population figures, the Englishes that were in contact in New Zealand (and on the boat during the long trip out) came from England, Scotland and Ireland in roughly the proportion 50:27:23 (see McKinnon, 1997). The north of England, however, was underrepresented. This tallies rather well with Bauer's lexical study (Bauer, 2000), which shows that there are focal points for the dialectal origins of New Zealand lexis 'in Scotland, in Ireland and in a band stretching from Lincolnshire ... through Nottinghamshire, Warwickshire and Somerset to Devon and Cornwall' (Bauer, 2000: 52). In keeping with figures showing the importance of immigration from the southwest of England, there are many instances of forms from this area, such as present tense *be*:

There be several.

and of *wasn't* pronounced as /wɒdn/.

There is also at least one grammatical feature on the ONZE tapes which is unambiguously of Irish origin. This is the perfective grammatical construction exemplified in:

He was after carrying 20 bags of wheat.

There are also many instances of Scottish forms in the ONZE archive. As far as phonology is concerned, the *Scottish Vowel Length Rule*, also known as 'Aitken's Law' (see Aitken, 1984), occurs in the speech of a minority of our informants. This is the rule which developed from the late sixteenth century onwards and spread out from the West Central Lowlands of Scotland (Johnston, 1997a: 67), according to which, while all vowels are basically short and there is no phonemic length distinction in the system as such, all vowels apart from KIT and STRUT are longer before /r/, a voiced fricative or a morpheme boundary than elsewhere. Because of the effect of the morpheme boundary, there is the well-known consequence (see Wells, 1982: 400) that *greed* and *agreed* do not rhyme and that *need* is not homophonous with *kneed*. Aitken's Law also gives rise to very different allophones of /ai/ (for further discussion of complications see Chapter 4), such that the first element of the PRICE vowel in *tight, tide* is much closer [təɪd] than the first element in *tie, tied* [taed].

Other Scottish phonological features include the fact that a number of informants also preserve as distinct the KIT vowel in *first*, the STRUT vowel in *fur*, and the DRESS vowel in *fern*. Others merely have *fern* as distinct from the other two, which are merged. This reflects a similar situation in Scotland itself (Wells, 1982). A proportion of speakers do not distinguish between the vowels of FOOT and GOOSE. Some of the speakers, in the Scottish manner, also have TRAP and PALM as not distinct – that is, there is no distinction between /æ/ and /aː/, with a vowel often of the type /a/ occurring in both lexical sets. Some speakers have [æ] in TRAP and PALM and [a] in START but this is an allophonic distinction with [a] occurring only before /r/. And, for a number of speakers, LOT and THOUGHT are not distinct. A number of informants employ the voiceless velar fricative /x/ in placenames and surnames such as *Cochrane* and in the exclamation *och!*. And a number of our speakers demonstrate an assimilation of /r/ and /s/ into retroflex [ʂ] in items such as *first, worse*. (This feature is often associated with the Gaelic or formerly Gaelic-speaking areas of the Highlands and Islands but can also be found in Scots-speaking areas – see Johnston, 1997b: 511.) We also observe typical Scottish stress patterns, such as *recognise* with stress on the final syllable (Aitken, 1984).

We also have a number of grammatical forms which are clearly of Scottish origin, such as the plural of *sheaf* as *sheafs*. And, in the syntax, we find some speakers who use, even in colloquial speech, nominal rather than verbal negation and who say, for example,

They had no ploughs.
They would get no food.

rather than *They didn't have any ploughs* and *They wouldn't get any food*, something I also take to be Scottish rather than English English in origin (see Aitken, 1984). The use of *for* as a conjunction, as in

For he liked it very much

is also likely to be Scottish in origin.

Another particularly interesting regional feature concerns what some writers have referred to as the Northern Agreement Rule: 'When the subject is a noun, adjective, interrogative or relative pronoun, or when the verb and subject are separated by a clause, the verb takes the termination -s in all persons' (Murray, 1873: 211). This rule is operative in the Traditional-dialects (in the sense of Wells, 1982: 4) of northern England, Scotland and northern Ireland. One of its consequences is that plural subjects take present tense verb forms with 'plural' zero endings only if they are pronominal. This is apparent also in the past tense but, obviously, only in the case of the verb *to be*. In our corpus we have speakers who say, for example,

The roads was bad.

but

They were really bad.

but we have no instances on the recordings from the present tense. (The narrative content of many of the interviews on our tapes makes for a bias against present-tense forms, of course.) We can suppose an origin here from outside England (i.e. from Scotland), in view of the rarity of other north of England forms.

To this New Zealand evidence, we can also add some data from Australia. In Trudgill (1986b), I argued that the mixed nature of Australian English is very clear from the role that Irish English played in its formation. It is true that Irish English phonological influence is not immediately apparent, although I do suggest there that the 'the Australian tendency actually to release word-final /p, t, k/, often together with some aspiration, is due to the influence of certain British Isles varieties [including] Ireland'. (I shall argue below that there was a more important if now concealed phonological contribution to Australian English from Irish English: since Irish immigrants were in a minority in Australia, we would expect, according to the thesis developed in this book, that their influence would manifest itself in phonology only if it happened to coincide with other regional British dialects, which, as I shall show below, is indeed the case.) However, because of extensive if minority Irish emigration to Australia, we should not be surprised if Irish English has left some other, non-phonological traces. I cite the following:

1. The presence in nonstandard Australian (and indeed New Zealand) English of the second person plural pronoun *youse*. This is very common indeed in Ireland, and for many speakers it is categorical. It is unknown in most of England, and is almost confined there to Liverpool and Newcastle, where Irish influence has been very heavy. In Scotland, it is most common in Glasgow for the same reason.

2. The grammatical construction exemplified in *Come here till I kiss you* – '... so that I can kiss you' – is not known in England except, again, in Liverpool. It is very usual in some forms of Irish English, and is also well known to many Australians as a nonstandard form.

3. Sentence-final *but*, as in *I don't like it but*, is well known in colloquial Australian English. It does not occur in England, except in Tyneside, but is common in Ireland and Scotland. Interestingly, it also occurs in the Falkland Islands (Sudbury, 2000).

4. Northern Irish punctual *whenever*, referring to a single event, as in *Whenever I was born, my parents were very poor*, is known to some Australians, but is unknown in England (Trudgill and Hannah, 2002).

5. The usage in colloquial Australian English of Irish and Scottish *It is so* as a denial, as in:

    It's time to go.
    It isn't!
    It is so!

contrasts with English English, where *It IS!* would be usual. This feature is also found in New Zealand English (David Britain p.c.).

6. Perhaps the most striking evidence of Irish English influence comes from the frequent usage in Australian English of negative epistemic *mustn't*, as in *He mustn't have seen me* – *he didn't stop.*

This is unknown in England, where *can't* would be used instead, except in Liverpool, but quite usual in Irish English (see Trudgill and Hannah, 2002).

MIXTURE AND SIMILARITY

Also in favour of the dialect mixture thesis is the following. I accept as obvious that there are many current similarities to be found between the Englishes of New Zealand and Australia. I also note, however, a significant degree of similarity between these two varieties, on the one hand, and South African English and Falkland Islands English, on the other. These latter two varieties have a significant number of features in common with Australian English and New Zealand English. In the words of de Klerk (1996), 'South African and Australasian varieties are clearly distinguishable from Northern varieties'. Wells (1982: 592) agrees and also includes the English of the Falkland Isles:

> The Australian and New Zealand accents of English are very similar to one another. South African, although differing in a number of important respects, also has a general similarity to Australian ... Interestingly enough, the brief samples of Falklands pronunciation I have heard were rather reminiscent of an Australian accent.

A number of the similarities betweeen the Falklands and Australasia are also reported in Trudgill (1986) and in Sudbury (2000), who cites many instances of Falkland Islanders travelling overseas being taken for Australians or South Africans.

These similarities, I maintain, are mostly due to the fact that South African and Australian and Falkland Islands English are, like New Zealand English, the result of dialect mixture, and that furthermore they arose from similar mixtures of similar dialects in similar proportions occurring at similar times. If you bake cakes, I suggest, from roughly the same ingredients in roughly the same proportions in roughly similar conditions for roughly the same length of time, you will get roughly similar cakes. (Equally, the English of Tristan da Cunha does not fit into this overall pattern of similarities –

which is clearly due to the fact that the mixture involved in its formation was *not* similar to that of the others: American English was involved, as was the creoloid English of St Helena, together with the language contact mentioned above.)

Note that the same point is made for North American French by Poirier (1994: 256) who points out that

> the process of linguistic unification, i.e. the fusion of different regional French forms into a single variety, took place independently but in a parallel manner in the three centres of French colonisation in America, Quebec, Acadia [the Canadian Maritime provinces], and Louisiana [my translation].

(On the other hand, a number of other writers on Canadian French have failed to see the explanatory possibilities of colonial dialect mixing as a process, and have therefore been forced to develop a kind of monogenetic theory in which they posit the existence in seventeenth-century France of a unified 'français régional populaire' – see the discussion in Poirier, 1994: 259.)

The 'similar mixture' thesis is also very much the view of Bernard who, writing in the *Macquarie Dictionary* (1981: 20), says that 'the ingredients of the mixing bowl were very much the same, and at different times and in different places the same process was carried out and the same end point achieved'. Bernard is writing here of the homogeneity of Australian English but I take this homogeneity, in fact, to be evidence in favour of the dialect mixture hypothesis. I argue, with Bernard, that the uniformity of Australian English is one of the results of the common dialect mixture and dialect contact processes which occurred throughout the country, and which led to the formation of Australian English in the first place. To this day, Australian English is extraordinarily geographically uniform. With the exception of the treatment of the lexical set of *dance* (see Chapters 5 and 7), differences are confined almost entirely to very small phonetic differences (Bradley, 1989) or to lexis (Bryant, 1989).

New Zealand English is also very uniform. The only phonological exception is that the Southland area of the South Island, around Invercargill and Gore (Bartlett, 2003), stands out from the other areas through its retention of rhoticity (and one or two other features – I discuss reasons for this retention below). Bauer and Bauer (2003) also discuss regional lexical differences in children's language.

In South African English there is, it is true, a small amount of regional variation: Branford (1994: 472) mentions differences between white speakers of East Cape origin; white speakers with a 'Natal' accent; and white members of the Transvaal working class; but we can note that this corresponds precisely to the three distinct periods of immigration (see below).

Observe, in support of the view that dialect mixture leads to homogeneity, the parallels with the development of American English. The results of dialect contact and mixture explain comments by observers in the 1700s to the effect that American English was very 'uniform' (Algeo, 2001). We do not assume that this refers to a total absence of regional variation – merely to the fact that European visitors did not encounter a phenomenon they were used to from home, namely that dialects changed their character very noticeably every few miles or so. Common dialect mixtures and levelling processes would have led to a reduction of regional variation.

Mougeon and Beniak (1994: 1) also write of Quebec French as 'a variety of French which is striking both in its homogeneity and its originality'. Asselin and McLaughlin (1994: 110) quote seventeenth-century reports that Canadian French was 'pure and without an accent'; and Flikeid (1994: 320) says that the evidence suggests that there must have been considerable linguistic unity very early on in the French of Acadia.

The same thing is true of colonial Spanish. Lipski (1994: 45) writes that the enormous diversity of Iberia

> contrasts sharply with contemporary Latin America, where even the most rustic and isolated dialects spread out over thousands of miles share a greater similarity (and almost total mutual intelligibility) than Peninsular dialects circumscribed by a tiny radius. This homogeneity is not recent; colonial documents reveal comparable levels of similarity among dialects, even at the vernacular level

and indeed Latin American Spanish was 'even more homogeneous in its embryonic stage, with major dialect differences developing in subsequent centuries'.

Dialect contact would also explain comments by observers in the 1700s to the effect that American English was 'better' than English in England (Algeo, 2001; Montgomery, 2001): one of the consequences of dialect mixing (see Trudgill, 1986 and below) is *levelling*, in which minority forms, socially marked forms and linguistically marked forms are lost. This is a feature shared by American English with other colonial varieties of the language. Turner (1994: 284), for example, quotes Bennett (1834) as saying that the English spoken in Australia is also 'very pure'. For Canadian French, Hull (1994: 183) describes the outcome of the social dialect mixture that took place as being 'mesolectal'.

In short, the evidence for the presence of a mixture of British Isles English dialects in nineteenth-century New Zealand and Australia is overwhelming.

THE SOUTHERN HEMISPHERE ENGLISHES

In the rest of this monograph, I therefore devote my attention to the one factor which I regard as having been, in most instances of colonial new-dialect formation, the most important – namely, dialect contact – and I attempt a more detailed examination of its role in the formation of colonial Englishes.

The evidence of the ONZE Project suggests that, in colonial situations, the development of a new unitary dialect out of a dialect mixture situation takes approximately fifty years (i.e. two generations): the first generation of New Zealand-born anglophones, e.g. the Mobile Unit speakers, do not speak New Zealand English. We can therefore suppose, very roughly, that Australian English was formed in the speech of those born in the period 1790–1840 (Cochrane, 1989; Turner, 1994), and we would therefore expect to find the first adolescent speakers of this fully-fledged variety in about 1855. Mitchell (1995) suggests a date of 1861, which tallies fairly well with this. Baker (1966: 431) quotes from a New South Wales School Commission of 1854–5 who complain about 'an Australian dialect', which also tallies well with our hypothetical date. Turner plumps for a rather later date, saying (1994: 285) that 'it seems that the outlines of Australian English pronunciation were established by the end of the first century of European settlement'. The process might have taken longer than fifty years in Australia because of the peculiar nature of the original penal convict settlements, with relatively few women present, and therefore rather few children. The 'first fleet', which arrived in 1798, contained 191 male guards and nineteen male officers, plus 537 male convicts. There were only 180 female convicts and about 100 officers' wives and children. Males thus initially constituted about 80% of the population.

We can similarly suppose that South African English was formed by those born between 1820 and 1870 (Lanham, 1996; Branford, 1994). We would therefore expect to find the first adolescent speakers of a focussed variety in about 1885. There was, however, regional variation in South Africa in the dates of first settlements: 1820 is indeed the date of the the first major Cape settlement, but, although there was anglophone settlement in Natal in 1824, the first major influx there was in the period 1849–51, when between 4,000 and 5,000 British people arrived (Branford, 1994: 434). In the period after 1867, there was another influx to the Transvaal, following the discovery of diamonds there. Lanham and Macdonald (1979: 22) agree that 'Natal and Eastern Cape have emerged as separate dialect areas from the analysis of the linguistic data' but suggest that the Western Cape might also, in some ways, be distinctive. If so, we can note that a relatively small number of English speakers first arrived in the Western Cape in 1795. Nevertheless, Lanham (1967: 105) is still inclined to allot a primary role to the Eastern Cape as 'the cradle of South African English', pointing out that 'even Natal had, in its earliest years, a preponderance of Settler descendants from the Eastern Province'.

For New Zealand, Bauer points out (1997: 386) that by 1890 there were more New Zealand-born Europeans in the country than immigrants, and he therefore concludes that one can probably take this date as a point after which the development of English began to reflect purely New Zealand trends. I agree with this dating, although we do have some speakers in the ONZE Project Corpus born after 1890 who have not acquired a recognisable New Zealand form of English, suggesting that speed of development would have differed from community to community. We know that, although English speakers first landed there around 1780–1800, the English language arrived as a significant force in New Zealand, with large groups of immigrants, only in the period from 1840 onwards. The crucial period for the formation of New Zealand English was thus between 1840, when the first significant numbers of New Zealand-born anglophones were born, and 1890. (The ONZE Corpus, however, has no data from speakers who were born in the 1840s.) We would therefore expect to find the first adolescent speakers of New Zealand English in about 1905. Indeed, Bauer (1997: 393) reports 'an awareness of an "Austral" pronunciation among New Zealanders (children in particular) from the turn of the century onwards', and tells us that it is from the early 1900s that public complaints begin to be made about New Zealand English pronunciation.

In each of these three cases (or five cases if we separate out the different South African settlements), subsequent immigrants would have been less influential as a result of what Mufwene (1991) has termed the 'founder effect' (see Chapter 7).

Falkland Islands English dates from 1834, at the very earliest, since this was when Britain established sovereignty. Of the approximately 2000 inhabitants of the Falklands today, roughly 80% live in Port Stanley, the capital. Anglophone immigration has been almost entirely from England and Scotland, although there has been some Irish immigration, and at least one settler from Bermuda (Sudbury, 2000). The population in 1850 was about 400, and by 1900 it had reached 2,000, although in the intervening period there was considerable emigration as well as immigration. There are two major islands in the archipelago. A distinctive local variety is present in Stanley and certain other areas of East Falkland. On West Falkland, which was not settled until the 1860s and where the population is very small, individual communities still preserve individual British Isles varieties, as mentioned above. In spite of the fact, therefore, that the Falklands were settled slightly earlier than 1840, when large-scale immigration to New Zealand began, it is likely that, because of the small population and frequent population movements in and out, (East) Falkland Islands English did not crystallise, to the extent that it has in fact done so (Sudbury, 2000), until later than New Zealand English. In what follows, I will use the term 'Falkland Islands English' to refer to the relatively focussed variety spoken in Stanley.

Schreier (p.c.) suggests that the dialect of Tristan da Cunha had probably achieved a fully focussed form by about 1880.

DETERMINISM IN LINGUISTIC CHANGE

In my examination of the formation of the Southern Hemisphere Englishes, I argue that, in tabula rasa colonial situations, dialect mixture and new-dialect formation are not haphazard processes. By 'tabula rasa' situations, I mean those in which there is no prior-existing population speaking the language in question, either in the location in question or nearby. I am therefore not making claims, for example, about new-town koinés of the type discussed by Omdal (1977), or Kerswill (1994).

I maintain that, given sufficient linguistic information about the dialects which contribute to a mixture, and given sufficient demographic information about the proportions of speakers of the different dialects, it is possible, within certain limitations, to make predictions about what the outcome of the mixture will be, at least in broad outline. I argue, that is, for determinism in this particular type of new-dialect formation. Indeed, it is this determinism which leads to the similarities between the Southern Hemisphere varieties that we have just been discussing. The similarities between the different and geographically widely separated varieties of English are due, not to any direct connection or contact between them, but to the fact that they have resulted from mixtures of similar dialects in similar proportions at similar times. But similar mixtures will only give rise to similar outcomes if the the new-dialect formation process is a mechanical one which applies in an identical fashion in all cases.

Linguistic change in general is, of course, not deterministic. As Lass (1990: 131) has said, 'no change is ever necessary. If it were, it would already have happened everywhere'. It is true that Mæhlum (1999: 172) has responded to the view of Harris and Campbell that a theory of language change 'can be predictive in the sense that we can state to an extent what the course of a change will be if it does occur, according to the universals' (1995: 6) by suggesting that this 'could be said to contain a certain element of determinism' (my translation). Nevertheless, historical linguists, including Mæhlum, are agreed that a theory of linguistic change cannot be genuinely deterministic in the sense that it is impossible for a theory to predict 'that a change will occur, which change will occur, when a change will occur' (Harris and Campbell, 1995: 321). I concur wholeheartedly with this point of view, and I accept Lass's assertion about the general inappropriateness of predictions in the human sciences, suggesting as they do 'an odd and untenably deterministic view of human action' (1997: 336). I do not even suggest that the outcomes of language contact and dialect contact are normally deterministic. My claim about determinism is made purely with respect to the unusual type of situation in which colonial varieties develop, in tabula rasa environments, out of dialect mixtures. Why should such situations be so very 'unusual' in this way? It is probable that what is most crucially unusual about this tabula rasa type of dialect contact situation is the absolutely pivotal role played by young children in the new-dialect formation process. Bernard appears to agree: 'The great likelihood is that it was the children of the first convicts and colonists generally, taking their speech variety from the community about them, who generated the first Australian pronunciation' (Bernard, 1981: 19), although the work presented in the present book suggests that it is actually the *second* generation of children who do the generating.

One thing we *can* confidently predict is that colonial dialect mixture situations involving adults speaking many different dialects of the same language will eventually and inevitably lead to the production of a new, unitary dialect. Our knowledge of such situations tells us that this is what always happens (unless the new community, as has been reported by Mæhlum (1992) for Svalbard (Spitzbergen), is very unstable). Although this is a very familiar scenario, it is not actually immediately obvious why it should happen. Why do speakers not simply carry on speaking like, say, their mothers?

The answer is that this eventual convergence of order out of chaos, on a single unitary variety, is the result of the fact that all human beings operate according to a powerful and very general maxim which Keller (1994: 100) renders as 'talk like the others talk', and which Croft (2000: 73) describes as being a reformulation of Jakobson's (1971) *phatic function* – that is, the drive to act out of conformity with social norms. It is this maxim which lies at the heart of the accommodation process (Giles, 1973), accommodation being crucial, as we shall see below, at certain stages of the new-dialect formation process. Keller's maxim, in turn, is the linguistic aspect, as I argued in Trudgill (1986a), of a much more general and seemingly universal (and therefore presumably innate) human tendency to 'behavioural co-ordination'. This is an apparently bio-logically given drive to behave as ones peers do, which is manifested already in parent–infant communication (see, for example, amongst a copious literature on this topic, Cappella, 1981, 1997). That is, linguistic accommodation is not necessarily driven by social factors such as prestige or identity, but is most often an automatic conse-quence of interaction. Of course, this drive can be overridden, as in deliberate linguistic divergence, but we can assume that acting as one's peers do is the unmarked case.

Normally, operating according to Keller's linguistic maxim is relatively unproblematical for young children who have not passed the critical period for language acquisition. Newcomers to a particular group automatically and quickly adjust to their peers linguistically. But, in a situation in which very many of the 'others' speak differently from one another, this is not a straightforward pro-cedure. So complicated is it, in fact, that the ONZE Project evidence shows that it takes two generations for all the speakers in a community to end up speaking as the others do, as noted above. Moreover, adults are normally able to go only some way in talking 'like the others talk', even in situations where all the 'others' talk the same. For adults, incomplete accommodation and imperfect language learning and dialect learning are the norm. There is no total consensus about language-learning abilities in the literature, but the view from sociolinguistics (see, for example, Labov, 1972) is that children acquire new dialects and languages more or less perfectly up to the age of about eight, and that the particularly complex phonological rules of a new dialect may not be totally mastered in complete detail even by children younger than eight (see Payne, 1980, and Trudgill, 1986a). In this type of colonial situation, therefore, where there is a multiplicity of 'ways of talking', we can suppose that most of the complicated work leading to the eventual establishment of a new, single norm will be carried out by children under the age of eight. In tabula rasa colonial situations, children of this age will be relatively impervious to social factors such as 'prestige' (see Chapter 7), hence the deterministic nature of the process, and the similarity of outcomes from similar mixtures. The process is thus mechanical or, in the terminology of Croft (2000: 65), 'nonintentional' (see Chapter 7).

Note that there is actually important linguistic evidence which demonstrates the key role played by children in many types of dialect contact situation. In Trudgill (1986a: 17), for instance, I presented data showing that phonological accommodation to another accent by adult speakers in dialect contact situations is inhibited in cases where a change would lead to the loss of a phonological contrast present in their own phonological systems, and I invoked there the well-known dialectological principle of *homonymic clash*. On the other hand, it is also well known that, in dialect contact situations, 'mergers expand at the expense of distinctions'. Labov refers to this (1994: 313) as 'Herzog's Principle', after Herzog's important work (1965) on the Yiddish dialects of northern Poland. How can we reconcile these two phenomena? How can mergers be favoured and disfavoured at the same time? The fact is that mergers are disfavoured by adults but favoured by children. And, of course, in the end, it is the children who win. Given that adults do indeed fail to accommodate when accommodation involves mergers, or at least resist doing so, then the winning out of mergers at the expense of contrasts *has* to be the result of accommodation by children.

Of course, in non-tabula rasa dialect contact situations, such as new town development (Omdal, 1977; Kerswill, 1994) and land reclamation schemes (Britain, 1997; Scholtmeijer, 1999), the role of children will not necessarily be so central, and processes will not necessarily operate in precisely the same way (though Kerswill at least has also pointed to the important role of children in Milton Keynes). This is because there will already be speakers of some form of the language either in situ – even if they are rapidly outnumbered – and/or in neighbouring areas, so that the normal processes of geographical diffusion of linguistic forms can take place. And in these cases there will not necessarily, either, be a complete break in contact with any normative traditions already established in the wider community (see Chapter 7).

I now proceed to attempt to demonstrate this determinism in new-dialect formation thesis, and to reconstruct the mechanisms at work in the original development of colonial varieties, through a detailed examination of the nineteenth-century English of New Zealand, as well as through comparisons with other colonial varieties of English, particularly those of the Southern Hemisphere. The difficulty which the time-depth brings to the detection of traces of dialect contact in North America and the Caribbean, of course, makes an examination of dialect mixing in the major Southern Hemisphere varieties of English all the more attractive, since they are younger than American and Caribbean English by as much as 200 years, and traces of the processes involved in their formation should therefore be much more visible.

Colonial lag and Southern Hemisphere evidence for nineteenth-century British English

The major goal of this book is to attempt to explain why colonial varieties of languages have the characteristics that they do. One of the objectives of work on the ONZE Project has been to try to answer the question: what is it about the formation of New Zealand English which has led it to be like it is? In order to answer this question, one must of course first decide what the distinctive characteristics of New Zealand English are.

The obvious strategy here is to compare modern New Zealand English to the English of Britain, whence it originally came, and to note the differences. In so doing, one needs to be aware that these differences may obviously also be due in part, as we saw in Chapter 1, to changes which have taken place in Britain but not in New Zealand since 1840. As Kurath (1972: 114) says, 'in the attempt to relate traits of a colonial dialect to the dialect of its homeland, changes that occur in the source dialect after the settlement must not be overlooked'. Phonologically, these late nineteenth-century and twentieth-century British-only changes include, amongst others:

1. the development of glottalisation, as in *match* [mæʔtʃ]
2. glottalling as in *better* [bɛʔə] (see Wells, 1982)
3. the lowering of the vowels of KIT, DRESS, TRAP (Trudgill et al., 1998)

Since moreover we are concerned here only with the formation (i.e. the origins) of New Zealand English, and not with its subsequent development, we need equally to factor out more recent developments in New Zealand English (i.e. those which have taken place since 1890). These include twentieth-century changes in New Zealand English such as:

1. the centralisation of the KIT vowel (see below; Trudgill et al., 1998; and Bell, 1997)
2. the merger, as a consequence of this, of the KIT vowel with schwa (Wells, 1982)
3. the ongoing raising of the DRESS and TRAP vowels to articulations closer than [e] and [ɛ] respectively, which is linked to the movements involving KIT and probably STRUT in a chain shift (see below)
4. the merger of the vowels of the NEAR and SQUARE sets (see Chapter 6; and Maclagan and Gordon, 1996: 131)
5. the vocalisation of /l/ and subsequent vowel mergers before /l/ (Wells, 1982)

In searching for the processes which lay behind the formation of New Zealand English, then, we need to look at the key distinctive features of this form of English other than those just cited.

I am arguing here that the Southern Hemisphere Englishes resulted in the first instance from contact and mixing between different British dialects of English. Any attempt to explain the processes which account for the development of Southern Hemisphere Englishes will therefore also need to consider what English was like in the British Isles during the period when the parents of the first colonial-born English speakers were born. For New Zealand, our interest is specifically in the English that was current in the British Isles when the people who were the parents of the first New-Zealand-born anglophones (such as the Mobile Unit informants) were born and initially acquired their native varieties of English – approximately 1815–1865. It was these varieties that they brought with them to New Zealand, and which provided the input to the varieties developed by their children, including the ONZE Project Mobile Unit informants.

We therefore need to look for evidence concerning these key linguistic features in terms of what can be deduced about their characteristics in mid-nineteenth-century British English. I take this evidence from two main sources: writers on the history of the English language and on nineteenth- and twentieth-century English dialectology; and the ONZE Project evidence itself, together with information about other Southern Hemisphere varieties of English. Since the speech of the ONZE Project informants represents a chronological period before New Zealand English as such had come into being, and since the nature of their English is in most respects the result of the characteristics of the English that was brought to New Zealand by speakers of their parents' generation (see Chapter 3), there is a strong likelihood that the ONZE data may give us some interesting and valuable insights into the nature of the nineteenth-century English of the British Isles. There is no problematical circularity here. It was a mixture of British dialects of English which led to the formation of New Zealand English, and the ONZE Project data enables us both to look back at the kind of English which left the British Isles with the first immigrants, and forward to the creation of the new distinctive variety which developed out of this mixture.

Of interest here is the notion of *colonial lag*. The American linguist Albert H. Marckwardt wrote (1958: 80):

These post-colonial survivals of earlier phases of mother country culture, taken in conjunction with the retention of earlier linguistic features, have made what I should like to call a colonial lag. I mean to suggest by this term nothing more than that in a transplanted civilisation, such as ours undeniably is, certain features which it possesses remain static over a period of time. Transplanting usually results in a time lag before the organism, be it a geranium or a brook trout, becomes adapted to its new environment. There is no reason why the same principle should not apply to a people, their language, and their culture.

Marckwardt is writing about North America, but I suggest that there is at least one sense in which 'colonial lag' (see also Görlach, 1987) is, or at least in certain situations can be, a demonstrable linguistic reality in most colonial linguistic situations. It is in this particular sense, moreover, a linguistic reality which can indeed be explained in terms of the transplantation of colonial societies, although I would hesitate to extend the notion to the social and perhaps especially the cultural characteristics of such communities.

Colonial lag does not, as I see it, require explanation in terms of adaptation to a new environment. I use the term here rather to refer to a lag or delay, which lasts for about one generation, in the normal progression and development of linguistic change, and which arises solely as an automatic consequence of the fact that there is often no common peer-group dialect for children to acquire in first-generation colonial situations involving dialect mixture. Thus, the models these children have are those provided by older people, and their speech is much more influenced than would normally be the case by the speech of their parents' generation. This type of lag must therefore, I would submit, have been a feature of early varieties of North American English which developed, as we noted in Chapter 1, in dialect-contact environments. I also suggest that this form of delay can on occasion have, as in the case of the data presented in this chapter, interesting methodological consequences for the study of the linguistic past.

The conventional sociolinguistic wisdom is that young children speak like their peers rather than, for example, like their parents or teachers (see Trudgill, 1986a: 220). This is necessarily correct since otherwise regionally distinct dialects would never have survived in the face of the increased geographical mobility of modern societies. In any case, the evidence for the thesis is overwhelming: in the context of families moving from one dialect area to another, the phenomenon of total childhood accommodation to the new dialect is the object of so much and such widespread observation and comment on the part of non-linguists that it does not really need scientific confirmation. American parents moving to London know very well that, before too long, their younger children, at least, will sound like Londoners. No one expresses any surprise, though they may express regret, if a Welsh-accented family moving to East Anglia quite quickly comes to consist of adults who still sound Welsh and young children who sound as if they have lived in Suffolk all their lives.

It is true that occasional individuals may be found of whom this is not true, but these are usually socially maladjusted, non-integrated people whose lack of linguistic accommodation to their peers is a sign of social pathology (see Newbrook, 1982). Payne (1980) has also suggested that, after a certain age, children may not master perfectly all the intricate details of phonological conditioning in a new variety they are exposed to, although the children she studied were in an area with an unusually large number of incomers. But the general trend is very clear: up to a certain age, perhaps eight, normal children accommodate rapidly and totally, or almost totally, to the speech of any new peer-group of which they become long-term members. This is the result of (a) the ability of young children to acquire new language varieties more or less perfectly after sufficient exposure, and (b) the tendency for human beings, ultimately biological in origin as we noted above, to 'talk like the others talk' (Keller, 1994: 100).

However, there are certain situations where this does not, in fact *cannot*, happen, at least in the short term. These are admittedly unusual situations where children are unable to accommodate to a peer-group dialect because there is no common peer-group dialect for them to accommodate to. Berthele (2000; 2002), for example, has investigated the Swiss German speech of a group of children at a private school in Fribourg in which, for religious and historical reasons, there has been a tradition of speaking Bernese German rather than the local Fribourg German, and where children come from a very wide range of non-local linguistic backgrounds, and thus arrive at the school speaking many different varieties of German, or no German at all. It emerges from Berthele's study that individual children adopt individual strategies whose eventual linguistic outcomes vary considerably, and include various degrees of mixture of different dialects.

Thus, because there was no common peer-group model in early New Zealand or the other colonies for children to aim at, a kind of 'colonial lag' occurred such that the Mobile Unit informants, because they were much more influenced by their parents' generation than is usually the case – though, as we shall see in Chapter 4, not necessarily by their parents themselves – actually give good indications in their speech of what the English spoken in the British Isles by people born as early as 1825 was like.

This can be illustrated by the fact that there are a number of grammatical features in the New Zealand archive which can be described as archaic in that we assume that they were more typical of mid-nineteenth-century English than of later periods. One reservation, however, is that a number of grammatical changes which have affected English in the British Isles in the last 200 years have started in the south of England and spread out from there, arriving later in the English north and southwest – and then in Scotland and Ireland, if at all – with some considerable time lag. There are a number of conservative features on the ONZE tapes which may therefore be either archaic, or English regional, or Scottish, or Irish, or all four. One such is the use of *for–to* infinitives, as in:

> *They had for to gather the crops.*
> *He wished for my mother to sail out.*
> *It was difficult for to get help.*

About 20% of the Mobile Unit speakers use this construction on the recordings, including people with parents from Cumberland, Cornwall and Gloucestershire. Another such feature is the use of the contraction *'Twas* for *It was*.

We can also note interesting phenomena concerning the verb *to have*. There are many instances in the ONZE archive of main verb *have* behaving grammatically like modern English auxiliary *have*. First, it may undergo contraction:

> *They'd no room.*

Second, it does not require *do*-support in negation:

> *If they hadn't enough ...*
> *She hadn't anything.*
> *He hadn't a situation.*
> *You haven't five pounds.*
> *I don't know how many roofs that old house hadn't.*

Crucially, this is true even when *have* has dynamic as well as stative meanings:

> *I'd an accident.*
> *They had a good time, hadn't they?*

In modern English English, dynamic *have* always requires *do*-support, with the sort of usage illustrated on the ONZE tapes now being confined to Scotland and Ireland, but this absence of *do*-

support was common also in England in the mid-nineteenth century (see Trudgill et al., 2002). As we shall discuss further in Chapter 6, there is probably also an ongoing trend at work here.

THE SHORT VOWELS OF NINETEENTH-CENTURY ENGLISH

We now return to a consideration of the key Southern Hemisphere phonological features in their nineteenth-century forms, looking at Southern Hemisphere English data including the ONZE Project data, on the supposition that the New Zealand Mobile Unit informants can provide us with information about the English brought to the colony by their parents' generation; and at the work of experts on British English dialects and nineteenth-century English generally. One of the goals of this chapter is to cast additional light from the Southern Hemisphere on the nature of nineteenth-century English in Britain: as Lass has said (1997: 205fn), to believe that nineteenth-century English was 'already modern' would be an error.

The vowels of KIT, DRESS and TRAP

England

The history of these three vowels, and of ongoing Southern Hemisphere developments, is intimately connected with the history of the English short vowel system as a whole. Middle English had a symmetrical short vowel system which consisted of five vowels only: /ɪ/, /ɛ/, /a/, /ɔ/, /ʊ/, as in *pit, pet, pat, pot, put.* This is the system which is still extant in the Midlands and the North of England, as well as in the long-term anglophone southern part of Pembrokeshire, southwestern Wales (Thomas, 1994: 131), and in parts of Ireland, including Dublin (Kallen, 1994: 176). However, in the southeast of England (Ihalainen, 1994: 261), probably starting around 'the end of the sixteenth century' (Brook, 1958: 90) – it is at around this time that 'foreign observers commented on the new pronunciation' (Strang, 1970: 112) – the beginnings of the FOOT–STRUT Split (Wells, 1982: 196) set in. According to Strang, in around 1570 the vowel /ʊ/ began to lose its lip-rounding so that a quality more like [ɤ] began to be more usual. This did not happen where the vowel occurred in certain labial environments so that words like *put*, *butcher*, *pull* retained their original pronunciation. This eventually led to a phonemic split between /ʊ/ and /ɤ/ (which later became /ʌ/), which was reinforced by the shortening of /uː/ to /ʊ/ in a number of words, giving rise to minimal pairs such as *look* and *luck*. According to Ihalainen (1994: 261), 'unrounded *u* was regarded as vulgar until the mid-17th century, when Simon Daines [(1640)], a Suffolk schoolmaster, described it as the accepted pronunciation'.

From then on, English in this southeastern part of the country had six short vowels, and it is not surprising therefore that the vowel of *pat* moved forward from /a/ to /æ/ to give a new symmetrical system with three front and three back vowels. Brook (1958: 91) specifically describes this fronting of /a/ as occurring 'at about the same time'. This movement continues to have consequences for the Southern Hemisphere Englishes, as we shall see below. The /ɔ/ of *pot* was also lowered to /ɒ/ as part of the same process (see Lass, 2000; Schendl and Ritt, 2002).

In the North and Midlands of England, on the other hand, /a/ stayed where it was, for obvious reasons. In the southwest of England, the six-vowel system did develop, although perhaps at a later date, but /a/ was not fronted. This is because [ɤ] was not lowered but rather fronted to [ə], giving rise to a symmetrical system with two central vowels.

/ɪ/	/ʊ/		/ɪ/		/ʊ/		/ɪ/	/ʊ/
/ɛ/	/ɔ/		/ɛ/	/ə/	/ɔ/		/ɛ/	/ʌ/
	/a/			/a/			/æ/	/ɒ/

North and Midlands	Southwest	Southeast

This is approximately the situation that we find in England today, although the phonetic details vary (see, for example, the discussion of the LOT vowel below). The Southeast system is also essentially the one found today in the Southern Hemisphere.

Scotland

It is necessary to consider the situation in Scotland (and related areas of northern Ireland) separately from England since the vowel systems in the two countries are so radically different from one another. At first glance, it would appear to be the case that the FOOT–STRUT Split is found in Scotland as well as in the south of England. This would be an intriguing phenomenon, as Scotland is, obviously, separated from the south of England by the English Midlands and the North, which do not have the split. However, it becomes less puzzling if a distinction is made between Scottish English, on the one hand, and the Traditional-dialect (or, indeed, language) Scots, on the other (see Wells, 1982: 395). (For an excellent discussion of the differences between the two, see Aitken (1984).)

Modern Scottish English, like modern Scots, has no distinction between long and short vowel systems. The monophthongs of Scottish English – they are all genuinely monophthongal – and their distribution over lexical sets can be portrayed as follows:

/i/		/u/	FLEECE		GOOSE, FOOT
/e/	/ɪ/	/o/	FACE	KIT	GOAT
/ɛ/	/ʌ/	/ɔ/	DRESS	STRUT	LOT, THOUGHT
	/a/			TRAP, PALM	

It will be seen that FOOT and STRUT have distinct vowels, as in the south of England. The situation is rather different, however, if we examine Scots, in which the medieval /ʊ/ vowel was also unrounded and lowered to /ʌ/. (This is also true of the very far north of Northumberland in England – see Map 12 in Chapter 6.) However, there are two major differences from the corresponding sound change in southern England which can lead us to suppose that the two changes, in England and Scotland, were unconnected (i.e. there was no diffusion from one area to another – an unlikely scenario anyway given that the north of England was unaffected). First, the change in Scotland was much later than in England: according to McClure (1994: 65), the change did not happen until the Modern Scots period, which he dates from 1700. Second, it involved *all* the words in the relevant lexical set (i.e. there was no blocking effect in 'certain labial environments'). Thus, words such as *put, butcher, pull* have /ʌ/. Words such as *wood, look, book*, moreover, have not separated off from the GOOSE set as result of shortening, so that no phonemic split occurred. The vowels of STRUT and of GOOSE simply remained distinct, although they changed phonetically somewhat, and no separate FOOT vowel developed (see Figure 1).

The modern Scottish English usage of /u/ corresponding to English English /ʊ/ in items such as *put, pull* – giving an *apparent* FOOT–STRUT Split – is the result of the redistribution of Scottish English words over Scots vowels because of influence from English English. No additional vowel has developed; rather, some words, e.g. *pull*, which have STRUT in Scots, have been reassigned to GOOSE in Scottish English because they have FOOT in English English. In fact, the vocalic phonology of Scottish English generally can be seen as basically the result of the vowel system of Scots having been overlaid on the lexical sets of English, something which I argue below and in Chapter 3, may well have had consequences for the phonetics of the modern New Zealand vowel system.

Scottish English and Scots both have a very open vowel in TRAP of the type [a ~ ʌ ~ ɑ]. However, in considering close realisations of the TRAP vowel, as in New Zealand English, we need to remember the point just made that the distribution of vowels over lexical sets in Scots is very different from what it is in English. For instance, many words such as *grass, after, marriage* (involving Middle English /a/ before voiceless fricatives and /r/) are not part of the TRAP set at all in very many Scottish dialects, and are pronounced instead with the DRESS vowel (see Grant and Dixon, 1921: 44). In some dialects, /ɛ/ may also occur in items such as *bad, had, mad, drab, bag, bang* (see more on this in Chapter 3).

As far as the DRESS vowel is concerned, it is worth noting that, in Aitken's Law long environments, /ɛ/ can be very noticeably longer than in any form of English English: *bed* = [bɛːd].

The vowel of KIT in Scots is rather remarkable. McClure (1994: 65) describes it as being 'somewhat lower than the corresponding vowel in English'. Wells (1982: 404) also says that 'in more popular accents it may be considerably opener and/or more retracted [than in RP]'. Indeed, after /w/ and /hw/ it has merged with /ʌ/, as in *wit* /wʌt/ (McClure, 1994: 65), and according to Wells (1982: 404) there may even be a total merger of the KIT and STRUT vowels in some varieties.

English English

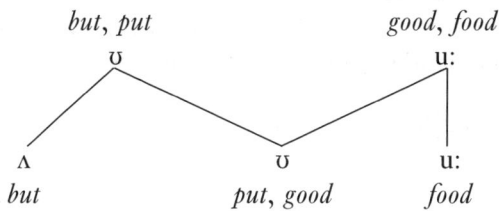

but, put   *good, food*
ʊ   uː

Λ   ʊ   uː
but   *put, good*   *food*

Scots

but, put   *good, food*
ʊ   uː

Λ   u
but, put   *good, food*

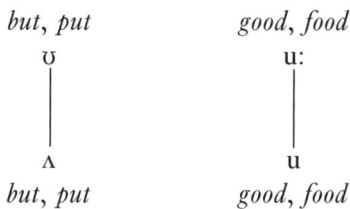

Scottish English

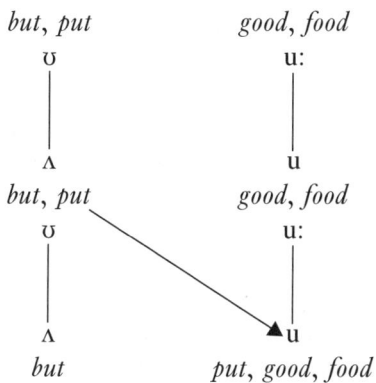

but, put   *good, food*
ʊ   uː

Λ   u
but, put   *good, food*
ʊ   uː

Λ   u
but   *put, good, food*

Figure 1: FOOT and STRUT in England and Scotland

Southern Hemisphere evidence

The phonologies of these different British vowel subsystems are reasonably clear. But what of the nineteenth-century phonetics? It emerges that the Southern Hemisphere Englishes can tell us much about this.

Modern New Zealand English is remarkable in having extremely close realisations of the short front vowels of DRESS /ɛ/=[e], or even closer, and TRAP /æ/=[ɛ], or even closer. In South African English and Australian English, these two vowels are also closer than in British English. Falkland Islands English has close DRESS but not TRAP. New Zealand English also has a very distinctive central realisation of the vowel of KIT, while Australian and Falkland Islands English both tend to have a vowel closer than British English; and South African English has both central and close allophones in complementary distribution – the KIT Split (Wells, 1982: 598, 612–13). Tristanian English realisations are not significantly different from modern mainsteam English English pronunciations, except that KIT has close realisations before /ʃ/, as in *fish, dish*.

A number of scholars, notably Bauer (1979; 1992), have argued that the New Zealand English short front vowels (and, by implication, those of the other Southern Hemisphere Englishes except Tristan) represent an innovation vis-à-vis English English. The argument is essentially that TRAP and DRESS moved as a result of a chain shift, most likely a push chain, which also involved the vowel of KIT. The lowest vowel of the three, /æ/, moved upwards in the direction of DRESS, forcing this to move upwards in the direction of [e] in order to maintain the distinction. Lass and Wright (1985) make a similar claim for a chain shift in South African English.

In an earlier work (Trudgill, 1986a), on the other hand, I claimed that Bauer's thesis (and by implication that of Lass and Wright) was incorrect. My argument was essentially that the Southern Hemisphere close realisations represented conservative pronunciations. Southern Hemisphere varieties differ from those in the southeast of England, to which they are typologically related, because the English English varieties have innovated by lowering originally closer vowels: [e > ɛ], and [ɛ > æ]. I proposed a drag chain for English English whereby /æ/ lowered from [ɛ] to [æ], which was subsequently followed by the lowering of /ɛ/ (and then /ɪ/). Current East Anglian Traditional-dialects demonstrate the first stage, where only /æ/ has been lowered, and words like *bed* and *hill* retain close pronunciations. This is also true of Falkland Islands English. Modern Cockney demonstrates the second stage, in which DRESS has also been lowered, but where KIT remains [i]; while other forms of southeastern English now have lowered variants of all three vowels. My argument, then, was that New Zealand English has not experienced this lowering and thus remains distinctively conservative with respect to TRAP and DRESS.

Very many of the ONZE Project speakers have DRESS as close as [e] and TRAP as close as [ɛ]. I suggest that this is confirmation of the presence of close vowels in nineteenth-century England. The modern New Zealand English close realisations were, I maintain, already present in the speech of the first- and second-generation of New Zealand-born English speakers – the close realisations were brought to New Zealand from Britain.

So the Southern Hemisphere Englishes have short front vowels which are close in quality (except, because of the later date of formation, for the TRAP vowel in the Falklands) because they inherited these qualities from southeastern English English, which subsequently distanced itself from them by acquiring more open qualities.

This conclusion is greatly strengthened by the fact that all four Southern Hemisphere varieties have much closer vowels than those of English English (except for Falklands TRAP): the occurrence of a single innovation – that of lowering in England – is very much more likely to be the correct explanation for this differentiation than the occurrence of four separate but identical innovations that just happened to take place at about the same time in four different and widely separated parts of the world.

We should also note, however, that there is one respect in which Bauer is certainly correct: data collected more recently from older New Zealand speakers (born 1934–54) and younger speakers (born 1964–74) show very clearly that TRAP and DRESS have become increasingly – indeed, strikingly – closer in New Zealand English during the last hundred years (Maclagan et al. 1999). (The other Southern Hemisphere varieties have not had the same degree of movement, if any at all.) That is, New Zealand English has indeed been innovative, although at a later date, in that these vowels have since moved in the opposite direction to that in which they have moved in England, with TRAP and DRESS becoming even closer as a result of a chain shift. Indeed, the movements associated with this shift are still continuing, to the point that tokens of the DRESS vowel are often misinterpreted by non-New Zealanders as tokens of the FLEECE vowel. (The modern New Zealand central KIT vowel is also a twentieth-century innovation, as we shall discuss further below.)

British evidence

TRAP

We have British confirmation for the close quality of the TRAP vowel in the southeast of England in the mid-nineteenth century. Ellis (1889: 226) quotes from a Mr D'Orsey who writes of London English that '*cab* is *keb*, *bank* is *benk*, *strand* is *strend*' which Ellis interprets as indicating a vowel around (E) in his transcription system, which is equivalent to [ɛ] (see Eustace, 1969). He also quotes from Field and Tuer's *The Kaukneigh Awlmineck*, which, in addition to writing *almanac* with <e> in the title, has many other words such as *bad*, *man*, *cat*, *rats* written with <e>. Again, Ellis interprets this as indicating [ɛ]. A German, Mr Baumann, is also quoted by Ellis as representing London English words such as *cab*, *catch*, *standard* with <e>. (Note that Ellis began his fieldwork in 1868.)

Similarly, Wright (1905: 22) shows much of Kent, Middlesex, southeastern Buckinghamshire, southern Hertfordshire and south-western Essex – the areas immediately adjacent to London – as having a pronunciation of /æ/ that he represents as **e**, which it is clear from his description (p. 15) represents a vowel which is actually intermediate between [ɛ] and [æ].

This supposition is supported by evidence from the SED (*Survey of English Dialects*). The SED does not, of course, provide us with information about mid-nineteenth-century English. But it is based on data obtained in the 1950s and 1960s from elderly speakers who were, in some cases, born as early as 1870. There is a large area of southeastern England where the SED fieldworkers often or indeed nearly always use [ɛ] as the transcription for the vowel in items such as *stack*, *hammer*, *apple*, *saddle*, *handle*, *rack*, *sack*, *mallet*, *paddock*, etc. Map 1, with data based on Orton and Wakelin (1967) and Orton and Tilling (1969), shows that this area straddles the Thames and includes all of Sussex, all of Kent and Surrey except for the areas closest to London, and southeastern Essex. The geographical patterning indicates that the area with this recessive feature used to be bigger than this – as Wright indicates – and almost certainly used to include London itself – as indicated by Ellis. There is also more recent evidence. Gimson (1962: 101) writes of refined RP and the popular London accent as raising /æ/ to 'approximately C [ɛ]' (where C stands for 'cardinal'). We also know that RP and other southeastern English English accents generally used to have closer realisations of /æ/ than is currently the case. Wells (1982: 129) writes of /æ/ that 'it is a striking fact that the current trend in pronunciation of this vowel is ... towards an opener [a]-like' quality, which 'is possibly to be seen as a reaction against the closer, [ɛ] type of realisation associated with Cockney'. The RP vowel is also clearly continuing to move in a more open direction. Gimson's 1962 diagram shows RP /æ/ as being about a quarter of the way from [ɛ] towards [a] (p. 101). Twenty years later, Roach's diagram shows it as being three-quarters of the way towards [a]. Indeed, Gimson specifically says that 'the quality is nearer to C [ɛ] than to C [a]', while Roach says that it is 'not quite as open as cardinal vowel no. 4 [a]' (1983: 15).

The suggestion, therefore, is that in the middle of the nineteenth century, regional accents in the whole area around London had a TRAP vowel much closer than [æ], and in some cases according to Wright, even closer than [ɛ]. Map 1 shows the area of England where the [æ] pronunciation – as opposed to the more widespread [a] – is extant in local dialects as portrayed by the SED, as well as areas where it is likely that close variants around [ɛ] were found in 1850. As we have seen, RP, or its precursor, is also very likely to have had such qualities at that time.

DRESS

It is legitimate to assume that close variants of /æ/ imply close variants of /ɛ/ too, and there is in fact evidence of close realisations of /ɛ/ in modern southeastern England from Gimson (1962: 101). Gimson describes modern RP as having a DRESS vowel halfway between [e] and [ɛ]. However, he also writes of 'that type of refined

1 [ɛ] in Wright
2 [ɛ] in SED
3 [æ] in Lowman
4 [æ] in SED

Map 1: The TRAP vowel

RP (and popular London) which realises /e/ in the C [e] region'. There is also evidence that RP and other southeastern English English accents more generally *used* to have much closer realisations of DRESS than is currently the case. Wells (1982: 128), for example, writes that 'old-fashioned types of both Cockney and RP tend to closer varieties than are now general'.

We also have some rather important indirect evidence from which we can *deduce* how DRESS was pronounced in nineteenth-century Cockney. This comes from modern evidence of how these vowels were pronounced in the (typologically related) English of East Anglia and other areas adjacent to the southeast in the speech of SED informants, who were born around 1870. This is very important evidence because it is very likely that many features of the accent current in London in 1800, although they may subsequently have been lost from London English itself, were still current in rural East Anglia in 1870. (One such feature which we know of is the use of /w/ rather than /v/ in *village, vegetable* etc. – see Trudgill, 2003; and Chapter 3.) The reasoning behind this point is as follows: for the last several centuries, it has been usual for features of London English to spread outwards geographically from the metropolitan area until they eventually take root in neighbouring regions (see, for example, Maps 2–6 in this chapter); this quite naturally takes time and, because of this time-lag, we can gain some idea of what earlier forms of London English used to be like by examining chronologically more recent dialects in neighbouring areas. The SED transcriptions themselves are in fact not detailed enough to be helpful at this point – the fieldworkers always write [ε]. However, their tape-recordings (supplemented by my own field research in this area) show that East Anglian informants (and this is still true to this day of older Norfolk speakers) employ pronunciations such as *bed* [bed], with close realisations.

KIT

There is also some evidence to suggest that the /ɪ/ vowel of KIT, which has shown 'considerable stability since Old English' (Gimson, 1962: 98), may nevertheless also have had a closer quality in some forms of nineteenth-century English English than that which is most current today. Gimson (1962: 97), for example, writes that 'a conservative form of RP may be much closer than the general RP /ɪ/

described above, coming nearer to the quality associated with /iː/'. This is true of many varieties of Cockney also. (Gimson transcribes the general RP pronunciation as [ɪ].) Modern West Midlands accents also have [i] rather than [ɪ] (Trudgill, 1986: 134): Wells (1982: 363) writes of Birmingham that 'phonetically, /ɪ/ is very close'.

Conclusion

My conclusion is that the modern close realisations of KIT in South Africa, the Falkland Islands, and Australia; the close realisations of DRESS in all four Southern Hemisphere varieties; and the close realisations of TRAP in South Africa, Australia and New Zealand, are a reflection of the situation in mid-nineteenth-century southern England. In the formation of the Southern Hemisphere Englishes, it was generally the early RP/southeast England closer variants of these vowels which were victorious, while the more open variants associated with Ireland, vernacular Scottish English, and the west and north of England, lost out. I will provide explanations for why this was so in Chapter 5.

The vowel of LOT

The modern Southern Hemisphere Englishes typically have a rounded vowel in this lexical set. However, some Falkland Islands English speakers do have unrounded realisations, and unrounded /ɒ/ in LOT = [ɑ] is very common in the ONZE recordings: 47% of the informants use an unrounded LOT vowel either consistently or variably. This suggests that unrounded LOT was formerly much more common in Britain than it is today. Wells (1982: 130) writes 'in Britain the predominant type of vowel in LOT is back and rounded [ɒ, ɔ]'. However, he goes on to add that we also find 'the recessive unrounded variant [ɑ] in parts of the south of England remote from London'. He further indicates (p. 347) that the vowel 'often appears to be unrounded in the west [of England], being qualitatively [ɑ], much as in the Irish Republic or in the United States'. And he also says (p. 339) that 'in Norfolk the LOT vowel has an unrounded variant'. Lowman's data (Kurath and Lowman, 1970: 22) coincide very well with Wells's suggestions, indicating unrounded vowels in most of the south of England apart from Suffolk, Essex,

Cambridgeshire, Hertfordshire and Middlesex. This typical pattern of geographical diffusion, with the southeast and southwest of England forming areas with unrounded vowels which are separated from one another by an intervening area, including London, with rounded variants, helps to confirm the Southern Hemisphere evidence that the [ɑ] area was much larger in the mid-nineteenth century than it is now.

THE LONG VOWELS OF NINETEENTH-CENTURY ENGLISH

Closing diphthongs

The modern Southern Hemisphere Englishes all have at least some closing or rising diphthongs – that is the vowels of FLEECE, GOOSE, FACE, GOAT, PRICE, MOUTH, CHOICE – which are characterised by Diphthong Shift. This term was introduced by Wells (1982: 256) to refer to the most recent ongoing developments associated with the Great Vowel Shift in which the diphthongs /iː, uː, ei, ou, ai, au/ show continuing movement of their first elements, beyond those reached by RP. Thus, /ai/ is the result of the diphthongisation of Middle English /iː/ in which the first element has gone from [i] through [ɪ] and [ə] and [ɜ] to [ɐ] and [ʌ]. Diphthong Shift involves more recent and continuing movement of the type [ʌ > ɑ > ɒ > ɔ].
That is:

- shift of /ai/ involves a first element backer than [ʌ], for example, *price* as in [pɹɔɪs];
- shift of /au/ involves a first element fronter than [ʌ] or closer than [a], as in *mouth* [mɛʊθ];
- shift of /ei/ involves a first element more open than [e], as in *face* [fæɪs];
- shift of /ou/ involves a first element fronter and/or more open than [o], as in *goat* [gɐʊt];
- shift of /iː/ involves a first element more open than [ɪ], as in *fleece* [fləɪs];
- and shift of /uː/ involves a first element fronter and/or more open than [ʊ], as in *goose* [gɵʉs].

I have not dealt with the CHOICE vowel in this work.

In those regional British accents which do not have Diphthong Shift, vowel qualities may simply be those of RP. In the case of those accents which are more conservative than RP, monophthongs are normal for /iː/ and /uː/, and for /ei/ [eː ~ ɛː] and /ou/ [oː ~ ɔː]; /ai/ begins with a vowel of the type [ɜ ~ ə]; and /au/ with a vowel of the type [ɜ ~ ø] (see fig. 5 in Chapter 6).

Southern Hemisphere evidence

Evidence from the Southern Hemisphere Englishes suggests that Diphthong Shift was already in existence in the mid-nineteenth century. Of the core ONZE Project informants born between 1850 and 1889, a majority, 75%, demonstrate at least some Diphthong Shifting. If we look at this in more chronological detail, however, we see that, of the ONZE speakers born between 1850 and 1869, 68% have at least some Diphthong Shifting while, for those born between 1870 and 1889, the figure is a good deal higher at 81%. Analyses show, moreover, that the phonetic extent of shifting, as well as the number of different vowels affected, also increases over time. Work carried out for the ONZE Project (see Gordon et al., 2004) shows further that Diphthong Shift occurred in the following order: /au/, /ai/, /ou/, /ei/, /uː/ and, finally, /iː/. That is, there is an implicational scale such that, for example, speakers who have shifted /ou/ will necessarily have shifted /ai/ but not necessarily /ei/. Britain (forthcoming) also argues that shifting of /au/ came first and of /iː/ last.

I thus conclude that Diphthong Shifted vowels were inherited by New Zealand English from English English, but that it was really Diphthong Shift as an *ongoing process* which was inherited by New Zealand English rather than any vowel qualities themselves, since the vowel qualities do not remain fixed, and Diphthong Shift can be seen to be on the increase chronologically throughout the forty-year period covered by the Mobile Unit data. We shall return to this aspect of Diphthong Shift in our discussion of 'drift' in Chapter 6. Crucially, similar developments have also occurred in parallel elsewhere in the Southern Hemisphere. For Australia, the closing diphthongs 'reflect the development we have designated Diphthong Shift' (Wells, 1982: 597). For South Africa, the closing diphthongs have 'undergone a development similar to the Diphthong Shift of the south of England' (Wells, 1982: 614). And it turns out that this is also true of the American South; Wells's Diphthong Shift is, after all, precisely the same phenomenon referred to by Labov (1994: 202) as the *Southern Shift* 'which governs the vowel systems of southern England, Australia, New Zealand, South Africa, the southern Middle Atlantic states [of the USA], the Upper and Lower South, the South Midland, the Gulf states, and Texas'.

The Falkland Islands too have Diphthong Shift, but the situation is a little more complicated because of the presence of a phenomenon similar to 'Canadian Raising'. 'Canadian Raising' is the Canadian English characteristic whereby PRICE and MOUTH have radically different allophones before voiceless consonants than elsewhere – I suggest in Chapter 5 that this is due to *reallocation*. In the Falklands, Diphthong Shifted variants of PRICE and MOUTH occur word-finally and before voiced consonants, but not before voiceless consonants: we find [œʉ ~ ɜʉ] in *mouth*, *out* but [æʳᵘ ~ aʳᵘ] in *now*, *down*; similarly [ɐɪ ~ ɜɪ] in *price*, *right*, but [aʳⁱ ~ ɒʳⁱ] in *buy*, *time*. The vowel of FLEECE is [ɪi], GOOSE is [ʉʉ], FACE is [æɪ], and GOAT is [ɐʊ].

The English of Tristan da Cunha has Diphthong Shift of PRICE, together with a 'Canadian Raising' pattern similar to that of the Falklands, but, interestingly, it does not have Diphthong Shift of MOUTH. It does not have Diphthong Shift of FACE and GOAT either – and indeed FACE does not even have Long Mid Diphthonging, though GOAT does (see Schreier and Trudgill, forthcoming). FLEECE and GOOSE are genuinely monophthongal, and for older speakers GOOSE remains back.

British evidence

For traditional RP we are able to date the origins of the modern qualities of these vowels reasonably precisely. For the vowels of PRICE and MOUTH, the modern qualities of the first elements of these diphthongs in RP (i.e. [a] and [ɑ] respectively) are thought by MacMahon (1994) to have been achieved by the last quarter of the nineteenth century (pp. 464, 466). For FACE and GOAT, Wells dates Long Mid Diphthonging – 'the change in FACE from [eː] to [eɪ] and in GOAT from [oː] to [oʊ]' – to around 1800 in the pre-cursor of RP, although MacMahon (1994) cites references to it in 1711 for FACE and 1795 for GOAT (pp. 450 and 459). The slightly diphthongal variants of RP FLEECE and GOOSE typical of RP are described by Sweet for 1878 (quoted in MacMahon, 1994: 461).

In order to be able to date the origins of Diphthong Shifting beyond typical RP qualities, we obviously need to examine varieties other than RP. (Scottish English and Irish English do not to this day have Diphthong Shift, and so obviously did not have it in the nineteenth century.)

MOUTH

As far as nineteenth-century regional dialects are concerned, Ellis cites Diphthong Shifted variants of MOUTH as being typical of his eastern division, i.e. Bedfordshire, Buckinghamshire, Cambridgeshire, Essex, Hertfordshire, Huntingdonshire, Middlesex, Norfolk, Northamptonshire, Rutland and Suffolk. (Note, however, that such forms have still not reached northeastern Norfolk – see Trudgill, 1974.) Lowman (Kurath and Lowman, 1970), who carried out fieldwork in England in the late 1930s, shows a rather larger area for this. And the area which has predominantly shifted forms in the SED materials is even larger. Diphthong Shifting in MOUTH in regional dialects at different periods is shown in Map 2.

PRICE

Ellis (1889) states that, at the period when he is writing, Diphthong-Shifted forms of PRICE are typical only of London. Map 3 shows areas which have predominantly Diphthong-Shifted forms, with first elements indicated by [ɑ] or [ɔ], in the SED materials. It can be seen that spread outwards from London has been rather rapid and that there are a few peripheral areas which have shifted MOUTH without having shifted PRICE and vice versa.

GOAT and FACE

Diphthong Shift of GOAT and FACE must logically have been preceded chronologically by Long Mid Diphthonging (Wells, 1982: 210), which was what turned these two vowels into diphthongs in the first place. We can therefore be sure that places which did not have Long Mid Diphthonging in the mid-nineteenth century did not have Diphthong Shift of these vowels either. It is remarkable that, in nineteenth-century regional dialects as shown in Ellis, Long

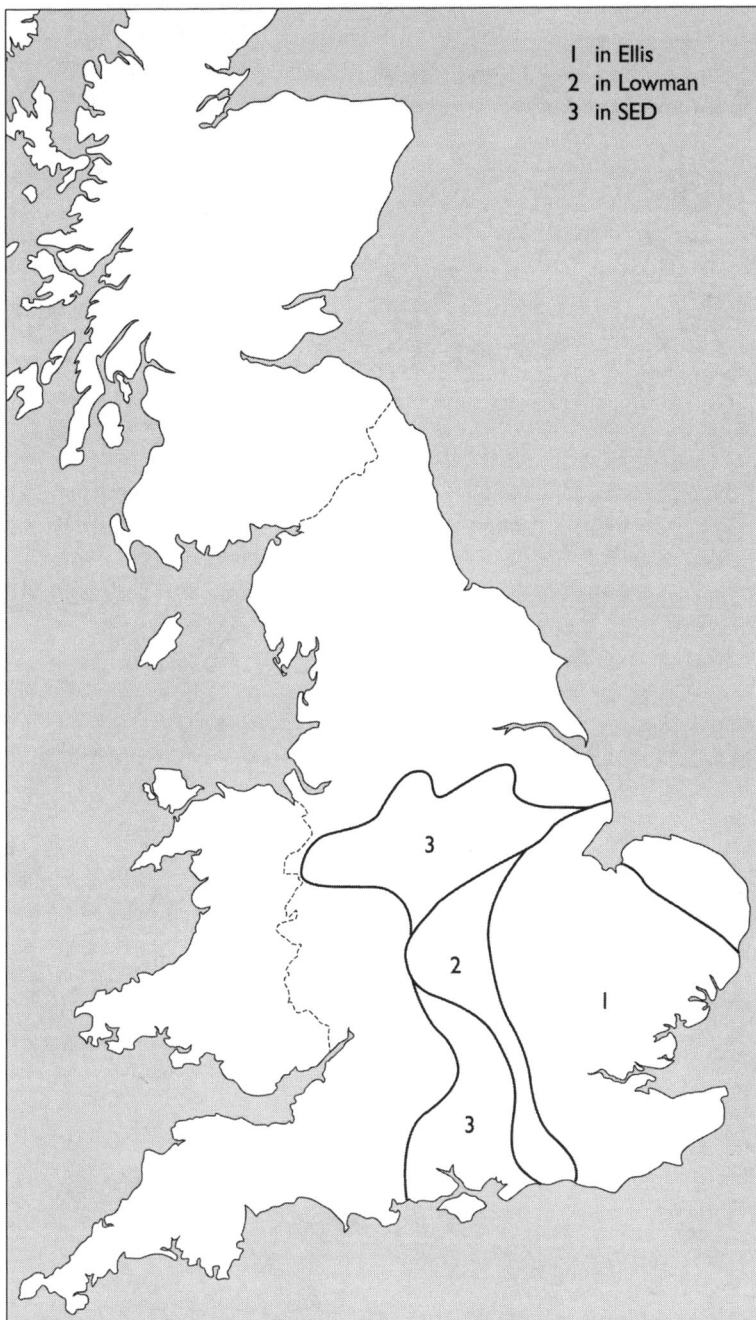

Map 2: Diphthong Shift in MOUTH

Legend on map:
1 in Ellis
2 in Lowman
3 in SED

Map 3: Diphthong Shift in PRICE in SED

Mid Diphthonging as a process had barely begun. (Indeed, very many dialects in all parts of England are shown here as having falling diphthongs, such as [fɪəs, gʊət].) Of course, there would probably have been more diphthonging in urban speech and at higher social class levels: Ellis refers to the rising diphthongs as typically a London feature. (Note that, as is still true of some twenty-first-century varieties, the vowels of the sets of *made* and *maid* and of *moan* and *mown* were distinct in many nineteenth-century dialects, the former member of each pair being descended from the Middle English monophthongs long *a* and long open *o* respectively, the latter from the Middle English diphthongs *ai* and *ou*. Long Mid Diphthonging is relevant, of course, only to the former.)

FACE

Ellis says that diphthongal forms of FACE (1889: 226) are an innovation characteristic of the regional speech of Hertfordshire, Essex and north and east London. Map 4 shows Long Mid Diphthonging of FACE in the 1990s (from Trudgill, 1999), in the 1950s/60s (from the SED), in the 1930s (from Lowman), and in Ellis (1889). Map 5 shows areas in which Diphthong Shift of FACE to [ɛɪ] or [æɪ] predominates in the SED materials.

GOAT

Ellis cites diphthongal GOAT as being typical of (though recent in) the regional speech of his 'Mid Eastern' D 16 area, that is, Essex, Hertfordshire, Huntingdonshire, Bedfordshire and central North-amptonshire. Ellis also shows that diphthonging is more advanced for FACE than for GOAT, which tallies well with what MacMahon says but not with the New Zealand or Tristan data.

GOOSE

The vowel of GOOSE, as part of Diphthong Shift, 'shifts from [u:] to [əʊ], though usually with the competing possibility of [ʉ:]' (Wells, 1982: 257). (We not consider that fronted variants after /j/, as in *new*, where very many varieties have fronted allophones, represent Diphthong Shift.) I consider these two possible types of GOOSE Shift – diphthongisation and centralisation – as separate but not necessarily mutually exclusive processes.

Map 4: Long–Mid Diphthonging in FACE

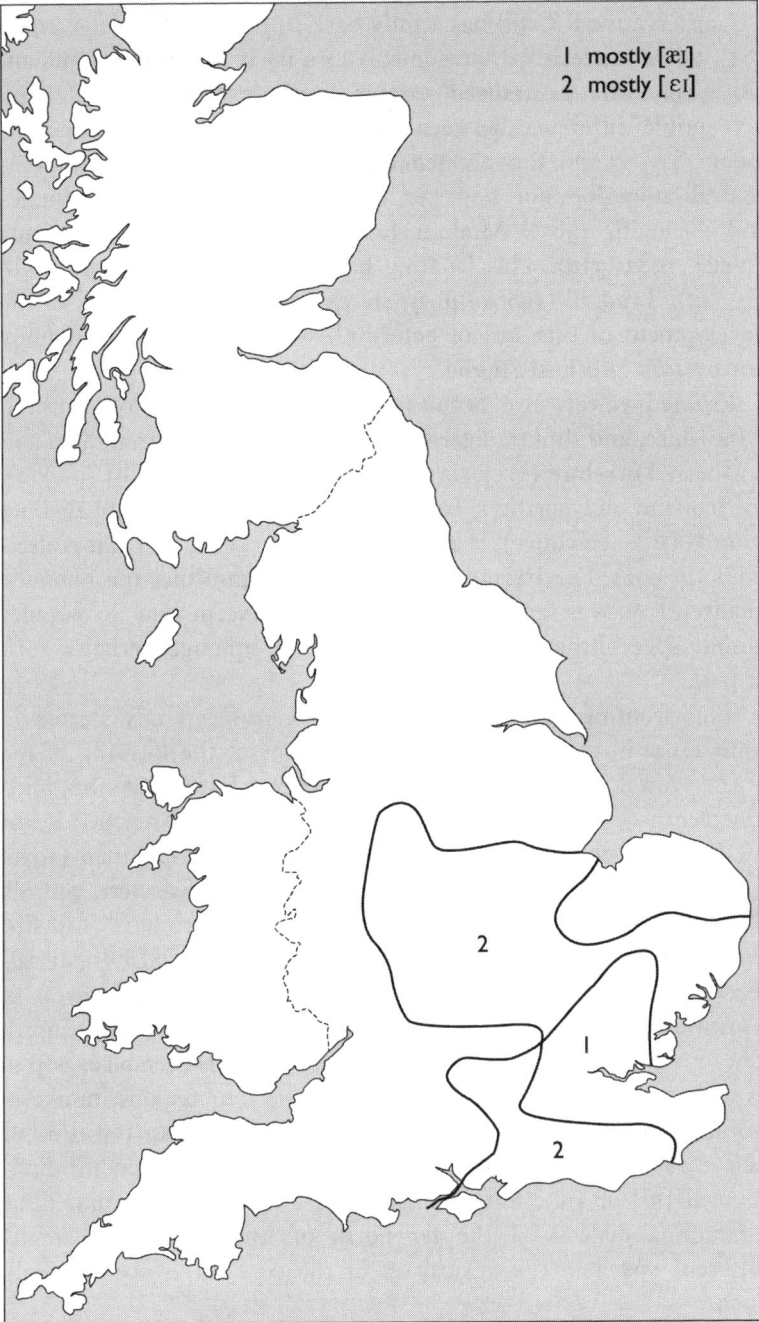

Map 5: Diphthong Shift in FACE in SED

Conservative RP still has a fully back [uː] in GOOSE (Wells, 1982: 281), while modern RP, presumably as a fairly recent development, has 'a somewhat centralised' variant, 'to the extent that there is no perceptible difference between the allophone used in the environment /j___/ and the phonemic norm' (Wells, 1982: 294). This centralisation does not, however, typically occur before /l/ (Hughes and Trudgill, 1995). Modern London also has fronted variants (Wells, 1982: 310). This fronting has also not occurred before /l/ (p. 315). Trudgill (1986a: 46–9) shows the ongoing progress of the development of this sort of before-/l/-versus-elsewhere allophony northwards into East Anglia.

Fronted vowels also occur in the modern accents of southern Lancashire, and diphthongal variants are found in Birmingham and northern Yorkshire (Wells, 1982: 359). Liverpool has [ɨʊ] (p. 372). In Scotland and northern Ireland (where this vowel is not distinct from FOOT – see above), it also typically has central or front realisations (p. 402). For Ireland, Wells writes (p. 425) that the phonetic quality of /uː/ is 'generally unremarkable' except that, in popular Dublin speech, there are 'some strikingly diphthongal variants' such as [ɛʊ].

This fronting and/or diphthongisation had certainly started in some areas in the 1800s. Ellis (1889) discusses the fronting of the GOOSE vowel as being a very well-known feature of the mid-nineteenth-century Norfolk dialect and likens it to French [y]. For the Traditional-dialects of the 1930s, Kurath and Lowman (1970: 13) show central vowel qualities for Norfolk and eastern Suffolk plus Kent and Surrey. Suffolk and Cambridgeshire have [ɪʊ]. For the Traditional-dialects of the 1950s and 1960s, the SED materials show extreme fronting to [ʏː] in Devon and neighbouring areas of Cornwall and Somerset, as well as in the south Lancashire/north Cheshire region; and there is centralisation in Leicestershire, as well as in Norfolk. It is noticeable that, in these four regions, unlike in London and modern RP, the front and central variants also occur before /l/. Suffolk and Cambridgeshire are given as having diphthongal [ɪʊ] or [iu], but not before /l/, where [uː] occurs. (The Traditional-dialects of the far north of England have a totally different vowel in this lexical set of the type [iə] – see Trudgill, 1999.)

FLEECE

We have very little evidence at all for Diphthong Shift in FLEECE from dialect studies. Map 6, however, shows the area with slightly diphthongal [ii] as opposed [i:] in FLEECE from Lowman's work in the 1930s. We can assume that this area is where the process must have started.

Conclusion

The chronological and geographical patterns shown in Maps 2 to 6 for nineteenth-century England confirm, for the most part, the evidence of the Southern Hemisphere Englishes. All of these developments involving the closing diphthongs, with the possible exception of GOOSE Fronting and/or diphthongisation, appear, from the configurations on our maps, to have begun in the English southeast; and, with the exception of FLEECE, they were under way, if only to a minimal extent in some cases, by the mid-nineteenth century. One can conclude that Diphthong Shift began with MOUTH and PRICE before spreading to FACE and GOAT, and then to GOOSE and FLEECE, and was brought to the Southern Hemisphere by the first anglophone immigrants. It also seems that Diphthong Shift of GOOSE occurred before that of FLEECE; but, for FACE versus GOAT and MOUTH versus PRICE, the evidence is conflicting.

The long monophthongs

START

The TRAP–BATH Split

The START vowel is a relatively new addition to the phoneme inventory of English and many varieties have not acquired it, including many of the accents of Scotland and the southwest of England where, for example, *lager* and *lagger* are homophonous (see Hughes and Trudgill, 1995). This new vowel came into existence phonemically as a result of the two lengthenings of the TRAP vowel labelled by Wells (1982) Pre-R Lengthening (p. 201) (which also affected PALM words – p. 206), and Pre-Fricative Lengthening (p. 203), leading ultimately to the TRAP–BATH Split (p. 232). Also involved in this phonologisation was R Dropping (p. 218), i.e. the

Map 6: Diphthong Shift in FLEECE in Lowman

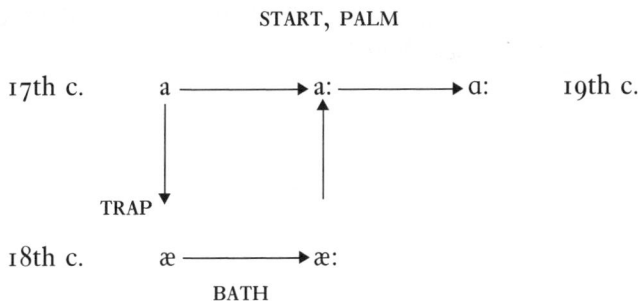

START, PALM

17th c.   a ⟶ a: ⟶ ɑ: 19th c.

TRAP

18th c.   æ ⟶ æ:
BATH

Figure 2

loss of non-pre-vocalic /r/. Pre-R Lengthening was the earlier of the two lengthenings and produced a lengthened version of the seventeenth-century TRAP vowel, namely [aː]; while Pre-Fricative Lengthening produced a lengthened version of the eighteenth-century TRAP vowel, namely [æː], giving START and PALM with [aː] and BATH with [æː]. At some time subsequent to 1750, the BATH set merged with the other two sets on [aː]. Accents in the north of England have not undergone Pre-Fricative Lengthening and thus have /aː/ only in the sets of START and PALM. (Lass (2000) has a slightly different scenario.)

The BATH set

The lexical set of BATH (see Wells, 1982: 133–7) has a number of different subsets and complications (see Figure 2). The bulk of the words in this set result from the Pre-Fricative Lengthening of the TRAP vowel just mentioned, resulting in /aː/ before the front voiceless fricatives /f, θ, s/ as in *laugh*, *path*, *grass*. As we have seen, this change did not take place in the north of England. (Neither, obviously, did it occur in those southwest of England or Scottish accents which, as we just saw, lack the /aː/ vowel altogether.) Moreover, a number of words, particularly polysyllables such as *massive*, *passive*, did not undergo this change even in the south. South Wales accents have /aː/ in *laugh* but /æ/ in *path*, *grass*, *nasty* (Thomas, 1994: 116). Another BATH subset results from the lengthening of TRAP before certain clusters of nasals followed by obstruents as in *sample, demand, plant, dance, branch.* However, there are many exceptions, such as *ample, grand, ant, romance.*

Southern Hemisphere evidence

In New Zealand, South Africa, Tristan da Cunha and the Falklands, as in southeastern England, /a:/ occurs in the lexical sets of START, BATH, including *dance*, and PALM. Australian English also has /a:/ in its inventory. The presence of this vowel in all four Southern Hemisphere varieties suggests a date for the development of /a:/ in Britain during the 1700s.

An exception has to be made, however, for the BATH subset which includes words such as *dance, sample, demand, plant,* etc. The Southern Hemisphere evidence suggests that the Pre-Nasal Lengthening which gave rise to this subset resulted from a change which took place *later* than Pre-Fricative Lengthening, possibly in the early 1800s. Many speakers on the ONZE Project tapes – 48% of them, in fact – have a split system in which /æ/ occurs in words such as *sample*, which involve a nasal, but /a:/ in words, such as *laugh*, with the voiceless fricatives. This system is no longer found in modern New Zealand English, although it survived in Southland until quite recently (Bartlett, 2003), but very many Australians still have it (see Bradley, 1991).

British evidence

MacMahon (1994: 436–8) dates Pre-Fricative Lengthening to 'a period of about fifty years' in which a gradual shift in favour of /a:/ took place, and cites Ward (1952: 95–7) as concluding that the lengthened vowels had become the norm by 1784.

As far as the *dance* set is concerned, MacMahon indicates that words with <ant> 'retain /æ/ beyond the turn of the eighteenth century' although lengthening in a few words such as *command* was earlier. Ellis (1889) shows /æ/ in *chance* in three East Anglian localities – Ely, North Walsham and Great Yarmouth – which certainly have /a:/ today. Speakers with certain Welsh accents (see Trudgill and Hannah, 2002; Hughes and Trudgill, 1995) currently still have the split system. (Wells points out (1982: 233) that Leeward Islanders in the Caribbean also have it while other West

Indians do not.) This would appear to be convincing evidence that *dance*-type words went over to the long vowel at a date later than the other members of this set.

START *Backing*

The current back quality [ɑ:] of RP and certain regional accents is a recent development which is due to START Backing, which Wells (1982: 234) dates to the early 1800s. MacMahon (1994: 456) argues that backing began amongst 'the lower sections of society' and suggests that a fully back vowel had become socially acceptable by the late 1860s.

Southern Hemisphere evidence

Modern Australian and New Zealand English, especially in their broader varieties, are characterised by very front realisations of the START vowel. This is also true of the Falkland Islands. This would appear to go against the early date suggested for START Backing in England by Wells. However, we do have to observe that START Backing is the norm in South African and Tristan da Cunha English. Unfortunately, we do not have any recordings of South African English speakers born in the mid-nineteenth century, so we do not know if this is a recent development or not. The absence of START Backing from Falkland Islands English, which probably developed later than South African English, might suggest that it *is* a later and independent innovation in South Africa. However, Lanham (1978: 153) indicates that backing may be a feature of South African English of long standing. If he is correct, this may be due to the settlements of the Natal and Transvaal anglophone communities at dates later than that of New Zealand – the additional decade or three allowing for START Backing to have become more common in urban southern England. It could also be due, if the backed variant had reached the upper-middle class by the appropriate date – it is certainly a feature of modern RP – to the greater role played by this class in the formation of South African English: according to de Klerk (1996: 10), the largely vernacular-speaking settlements of the 1820s were followed by the 'largely standard-speaking Natal settlements of the 1840s'.

British evidence

Map 7 shows the areas of England where back [ɑ:] occurs in the regional dialects, as shown in the SED materials. It will be seen that these areas are located around London and Birmingham. It might be possible, therefore, to argue that the South African puzzle can be explained by supposing that there was a higher proportion of immigrants to South Africa from the urban English southeast and the West Midlands than was the case for Australia and New Zealand. Hughes (2000: 306) indicates that, of the 1,658 families who constituted the original 1820 immigration to South Africa, 607 came from London and the Home Counties and 263 from the south or southeast, making up 52% of the total. Certainly, one of the small number of founding fathers of Tristan also came from London. However, I must concede that the Southern Hemisphere evidence is difficult to interpret in this particular case.

THE THOUGHT–NORTH–FORCE VOWEL

The /ɔ:/ vowel is also a relative newcomer to English phonology, and its occurrence and distribution vary widely from variety to variety. It is still not found in Scottish English. In RP and typologically related varieties, it has a number of different sources (see Figure 3).

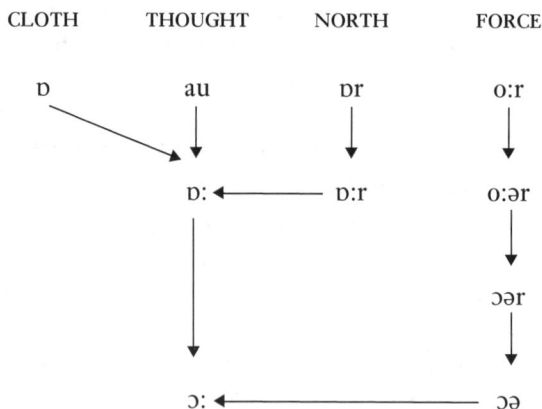

CLOTH	THOUGHT	NORTH	FORCE
ɒ	au	ɒr	o:r
	ɒ: ← ɒ:r		o:ər
			ɔər
	ɔ: ←		ɔə

Figure 3

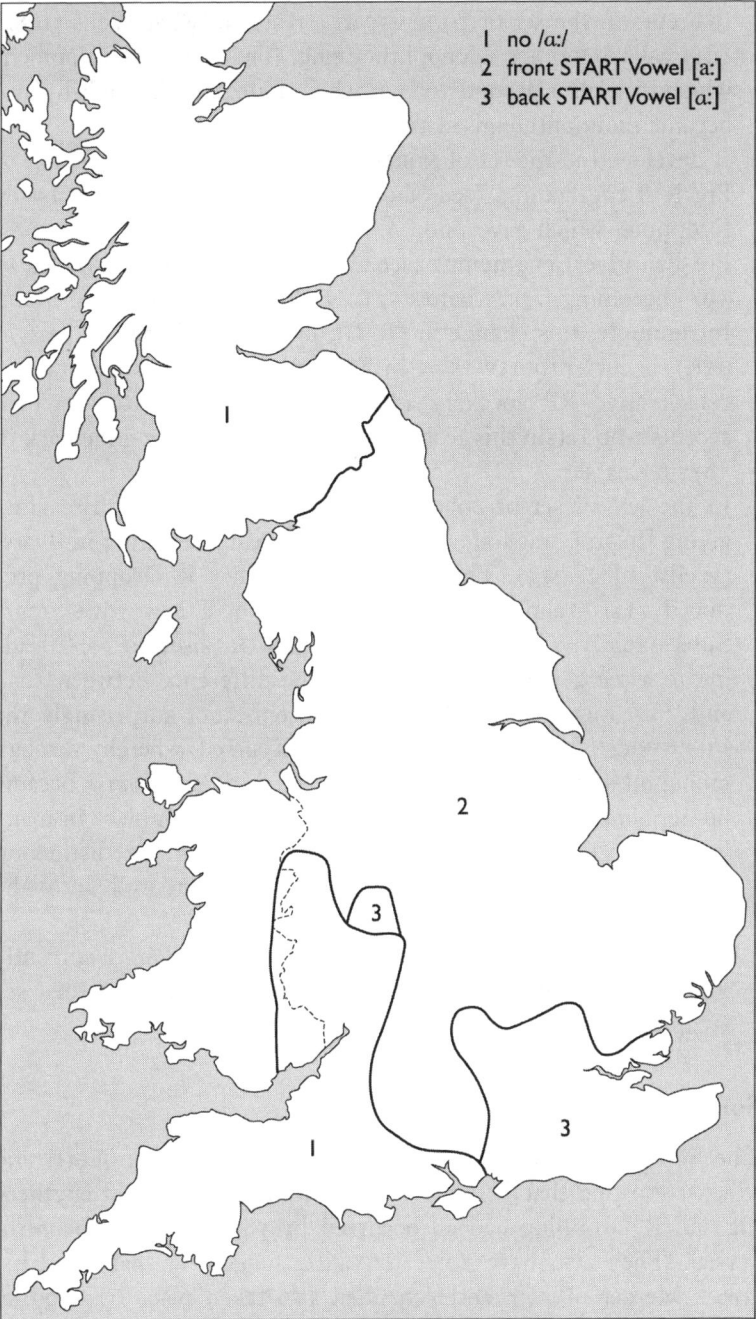

1 no /ɑ:/
2 front START Vowel [aː]
3 back START Vowel [ɑː]

Map 7: The START vowel in SED

1. It occurs in the set of THOUGHT as a result of what Wells (1982: 191) calls THOUGHT Monophthonging. This was a development which took place around 1600 in which Late Middle English /au/ became monophthongised to /ɒː/.

2. It developed in the set of NORTH, originally /nɒrθ/, as a result of Pre-R Lengthening (see above) to /nɒːrθ/, followed by R Dropping, which gave /nɒːθ/.

3. Pre-Fricative Lengthening (see above) in the set of CLOTH led to /ɒ/ becoming /ɒː/ before /f, s, θ/ as in *off*, *cross*, *cloth*. Intriguingly, this change in CLOTH, unlike the change to /aː/ in BATH, is currently reversing in England, so that it is now mostly conservative RP speakers and speakers of low-status regional accents who retain this feature, other accents having gone back to /ɒ/ in this set.

4. In the lexical set of FORCE, originally /foːrs/, Pre-R Breaking, giving [foːərs], was followed by Pre-R Laxing, resulting in [fɔərs] (Wells, 1982: 213). Then eighteenth-century R Dropping produced /fɔəs/ and thus the development of a new vowel /ɔə/. Subsequently, /ɒː/ in THOUGHT and NORTH raised to /ɔː/, leading to a merger with CLOTH. Since the difference between /ɔə/ and /ɔː/ was very small in many accents, not surprisingly the First FORCE Merger (Wells, 1982: 235) occurred, whereby through monophthonging /ɔə/ became /ɔː/ and *horse* and *hoarse* became homophones. This merger, however, has not taken place in many English accents, and indeed in conservative RP the distinction between THOUGHT/NORTH and FORCE survived well into the twentieth century.

5. There is now also a Second FORCE Merger, which is currently underway, involving items such as *poor*. For more on this, see Chapter 6.

Southern Hemisphere evidence

The Southern Hemisphere varieties all have /ɔː/ in THOUGHT and NORTH, showing that THOUGHT Monophthonging, Pre-R Lengthening and R Dropping had all occurred by 1800. This is uncontroversial. They also have /ɔː/ in FORCE, suggesting that the First FORCE Merger of /ɔː/ and /ɔə/ had also taken place by 1800, at least in some varieties of English English. This is perhaps more surprising since Wells shows that this merger was not completed in RP until the early twentieth century. Interestingly, in New Zealand, both vowel qualities have survived phonetically for some speakers, although the phonological merger is complete, with the diphthong occurring word-finally as [ɔə] or even [ɔɐ] (see Bauer, 1997: 389) as in *floor*, *flaw*, and the monophthong pre-consonantally, as in *court*, *caught*. (This is also true of London English.) In Tristanian English, the normal realisation is [ɔə].

The ONZE Project speakers also pronounce the lexical set of *off*, *froth*, *cross* predominantly with /ɔ:/ rather than /ɒ/, and /ɔ:/ is still today a good deal more common in New Zealand, Australia and the Falklands than it is in England in this set. In basilectal Tristan English it is categorical in all lexical items in this set.

British evidence

The SED shows the whole of the south of England as having /ɔ:/ in *off*, etc., supporting the Southern Hemisphere evidence that in the nineteenth century it was not only speakers of Traditional-dialects who had this feature in southern England.

THE CONSONANTS OF NINETEENTH–CENTURY ENGLISH

The phonology and phonetics of /r/

Rhoticity

Many modern accents of English are *non-rhotic*. That is, /r/ occurs only in prevocalic position, as in *rat*, *trap*, *carry*, *car appliance*, but not in non-prevocalic position, as in *cart*, *car wash*, *car*. This non-rhoticity is obviously the result of the sound change which Wells (1982: 218) labels R Dropping, and which is well known to have begun in England (Scotland and Ireland remain rhotic to this day).

The chronology of this change is of considerable interest. Wells (1982: 218) dates it to 'the eighteenth century, when /r/ disappeared before a consonant or in absolute final position'. Strang (1970: 112) claims that 'in post-vocalic position, finally or pre-consonantally, /r/ was weakened in articulation in the 17c and reduced to a vocalic segment early in the 18c'. Bailey (1996: 100)

writes that in English English 'the shift from consonantal to vocalic
r, though sporadic earlier, gathered force at the end of the
eighteenth century'. Walker (1791) states that non-prevocalic /r/ is
'sometimes entirely sunk', which means that the dates given by
Strang and Bailey seem to be accurate for London.

Southern Hemisphere evidence

Except for the Southland area, New Zealand English today is non-
rhotic (Wells, 1982: 606). Australian, Tristanian and Port Stanley
Falkland Islands English are also non-rhotic, as is South African
English (except for some people who are native Afrikaans speakers –
Wells, 1982: 617). This has often been erroneously ascribed (for
instance, in Trudgill, 1986a) to the fact that most of England was
non-rhotic at the time of the main immigration to New Zealand. It
is now obvious that this is not correct at all: of the eighty-four
Mobile Unit speakers analysed, an astonishing 92% are rhotic to
some degree.

This suggests that, in spite of the claims of Bailey and Strang,
rhoticity must have been very common in nineteenth-century
Britain; and that it has subsequently been lost in parallel in England
and in New Zealand. English English and New Zealand English,
having both been very rhotic in the nineteenth century, both became
very non-rhotic in the twentieth century, with the respective
exceptions of the English southwest and parts of the northwest, and
of New Zealand Southland, as a result of parallel developments (for
more on parallel developments, see Chapter 6). New Zealand English
perhaps therefore did not inherit non-rhoticity from English
English as such but rather inherited an ongoing process involving
loss of rhoticity. Given that New Zealand was settled later than
Australia and South Africa, which are also non-rhotic, I am happy
to assert that Australian and South African English must also have
been rather rhotic at one stage. Indeed, Branford cites evidence
(1994: 436) for rhoticity in South African English in the form of
early borrowings from English into Xhosa: for example, in *tichela*
'teacher', the /l/ corresponds to English /r/, indicating a rhotic
pronunciaton in the English of the time. As noted above, Falkland
Islands English is also non-rhotic, in spite of the fact that, as
Sudbury (2000: 93) points out, most settlement was from rhotic

areas of Britain, so it is quite possible that non-rhoticity here is also the result of parallel development.

British evidence

I have just asserted, on the basis of New Zealand evidence, that England must have been 'very rhotic in the nineteenth century'. Happily, there is British evidence for this also. For example, Hallam (in MacMahon, 1983: 28) provides evidence that rhoticity was a feature of some upper-class speech into the 1870s, pointing to the accents of Disraeli (b. 1804) and Prince Leopold (b. 1853), the fourth son of Queen Victoria (see also the discussion in Lass, 1997: 6.2). Beal (1999: 7–8) claims that Walker (1791), in saying that /r/ is 'sometimes entirely sunk', is referring 'only to the most advanced dialect' of his day – colloquial London English. She goes on to state that the loss of /r/ was still stigmatised in the first decades of the 1800s.

Dialectological evidence clearly shows that most regional accents were more conservative than London English and the prestige norm that was to become RP. Thus Bailey's (1996: 102) statement that 'resistance to the spreading London fashion was, however, not long sustained' cannot be seen as accurate as far as regional accents are concerned. Map 8 shows areas of England which were rhotic in different ways at different periods in local dialects.

As can be seen from data in the three major sources, there are only two areas of England for which we have *no* evidence of rhoticity in the mid-nineteenth century. The first such area runs from the North Riding of Yorkshire south through the Vale of York into north and central Lincolnshire, nearly all of Nottinghamshire, and adjacent areas of Derbyshire, Leicestershire and Staffordshire. The second includes all of Norfolk, western Suffolk and Essex, eastern Cambridgeshire and Hertfordshire, Middlesex, and northern Surrey and Kent. (There was possibly a third area in recently anglophone areas of South Wales.)

The phonetics of /r/

In modern Britain, five different phonetic realisations of /r/ are extant. These are:

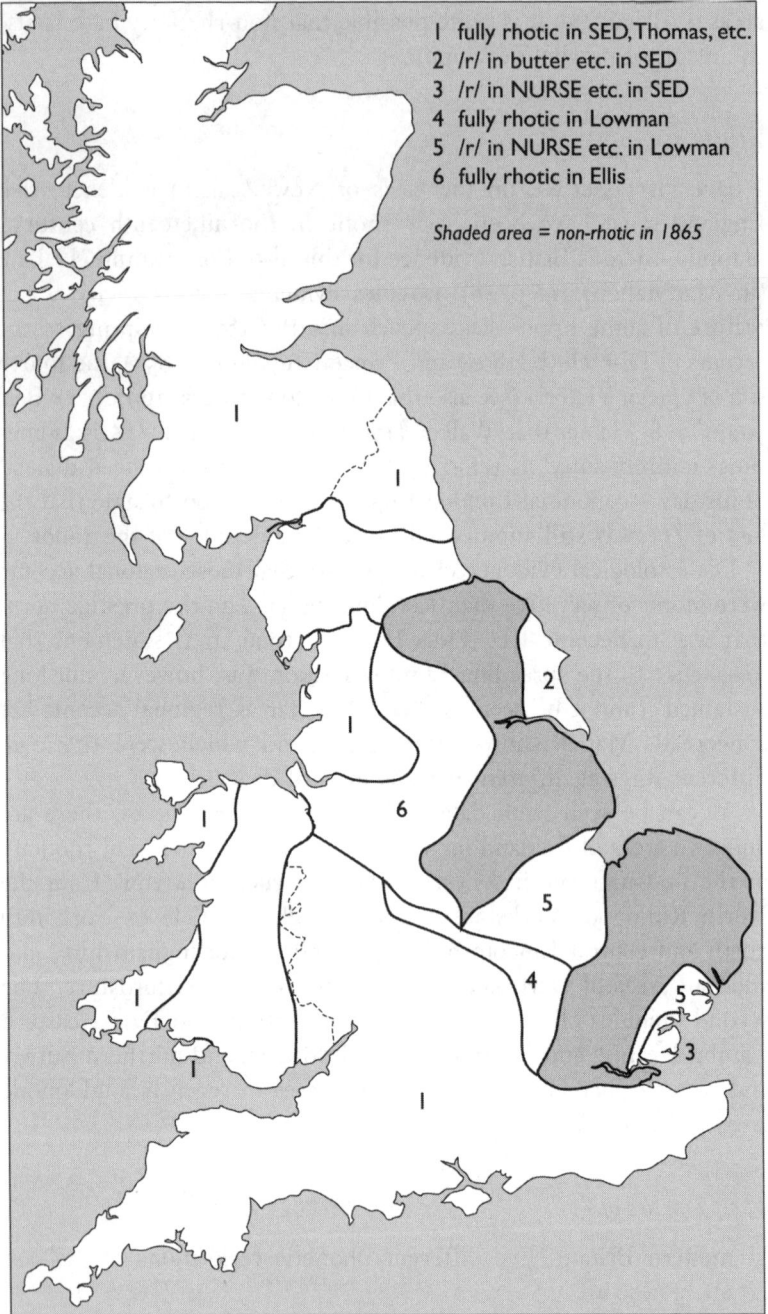

Map 8: Rhoticity

1. the sharply recessive voiced *uvular fricative* [ʀ], which is confined to the northeast of England (see Wells, 1982: 368) and some Scottish idiolects (Aitken, 1984);
2. the *alveolar flap* [ɾ], which is today usually associated with Scotland and parts of the north of England;
3. the *retroflex approximant* [ɻ], which is most typical of southwestern England (Wells, 1982: 342);
4. the *postalveolar approximant* [ɹ], most usually associated with RP and much of south and central England;
5. and the *labio-dental approximant* [ʋ], which is currently gaining ground very rapidly amongst younger speakers (see Trudgill, 1988).

There is no doubt at all that the labio-dental approximant is a very new pronunciation. Of the other three widespread variants, we can suppose on phonetic grounds – what we are witnessing is an ongoing process of lenition – that the flap is the oldest and the postalveolar approximant the newest, with the retroflex variant being chronologically intermediate. We can suppose that even earlier forms of English may have had a roll (trill). Bailey (1996: 99) indicates that 'weakening of r from a trilled consonant was first reported in Britain at the end of the sixteenth century' (see also Wells, 1982: 370). This gives us a history of lenition in the realisation of /r/ as follows:

[r > ɾ > ɻ > ɹ > ʋ]

Southern Hemisphere evidence

The relative chronology is clear; what is less certain is the absolute chronology. When, for example, did the variant [ɹ] become the most usual and widespread variant? Here the ONZE recordings are of considerable interest. The normal pronunciation of /r/ in New Zealand today is also, as in most of England, [ɹ], although on average this is rather more retroflexed, i.e. conservative, than in England. Australian, Tristanian and Falkland Islands English also shows more retroflexion than southeastern England. However, analysis of the ONZE tapes shows that the pronunciation of /r/ as a flapped [ɾ] is extremely common on these recordings. There is thus a strong suggestion that the weakening of the flap to an approximant in the South and Midlands of England is a very recent phenomenon, dating from approximately the middle of the nineteenth century, a development that has been followed, more or less simultaneously, in New Zealand. It is also of considerable interest that one of the ONZE Project informants, Mr Eccles, who was born and lived in Tasmania, Australia, until he was twenty, and who is therefore not included amongst the core speakers, has flapped /r/ too, suggesting that Australian English has undergone the same process. Some forms of South African English still have a tap to this day, which, as argued for by Lass (1997: 206), further strengthens this supposition (a trilled variant can also be heard, but not from native speakers – Wells, 1982: 617). Lass concurs that 'non-approximant /r/ is the norm not only for Scots, but for virtually all of rural England in the mid-nineteenth century, and for many towns and cities as well'.

H Dropping

H Dropping is the loss of word-initial /h/ in words such as *hill*, *house*, *hammer*, with the result that pairs such as *ill* and *hill* become homophonous. Not to be considered as H Dropping – *pace* Bell and Holmes (1992) – is the absence of /h/ in unstressed grammatical words such as *him*, *his*, *he*, *her*, *have*, *has*, *had*, where all English speakers lack /h/. Neither can we call the absence of /h/ H Dropping in words which have orthographic <h> but which were borrowed from French without /h/, such as *heir*, *hour*, *honest*, *honour* and where, again, no English speakers have /h/. However, care has to be taken in analysing the speech of older speakers with a number of words in this category which used to lack /h/ but now have it, as a result of spelling pronunciation – for example, *hotel*, *hospital*, *humble*, *humour*, *herb* (though American English still lacks /h/ in this latter item). Other words in this class (see MacMahon, 1994: 477–8; Wells, 1982: 255) have had /h/ for so long that pronunciations of them without /h/ can now safely be considered H Dropping: *habit*, *heritage*, *homage*, *hospitable*, *host(ess)*, *human*. Care also has to be taken with older speakers in the case of words such as *hotel*, *historic*, *hysteria* which have unstressed first syllables and which were treated, in archaic RP, like the unstressed forms of h-initial grammatical words – that is, they lacked /h/ also (see

Wells, 1982: 286). A final group of words in which absence of /h/ cannot be considered H Dropping because no English speakers employ /h/ in such words (Gimson, 1962: 186) consists of certain words with medial <h>, such as *exhaust, exhilarate, exhibit, vehicle, vehement, shepherd* (plus, at least in Britain, place names such as *Durham, Birmingham*).

H Dropping represents the end-point of a very long historical process in which the original Old English phoneme /h ~ x/ was gradually subjected to more and more phonotactic restrictions. It was lost word-initially before /r/ as in *hring* = *ring*, before /l/ as in *hlāf* = *loaf*, and before /n/ as in *hnutu* = *nut* in late Old English or early Middle English; in other preconsonantal positions during the 1300s after back vowels as in *daughter, brought*, and during the 1400s after other vowels as in *night, sigh*, at least in the south of England (McLaughlin, 1970: 110). The loss before /w/, as in *which*, is much more recent, and many varieties remain unaffected (see below). And the loss in absolute initial position, as in *hill*, is more recent still; Sweet (1888: 259) dates it to the late 1700s: 'initial *h* began to be dropt everywhere in colloquial speech towards the end of thMn [= third Modern period = 1700–1800]'. This would place it about twenty-five to fifty years before the beginning of the period in which we are interested. Milroy (1983), however, has argued that it is a much older development than suggested by Sweet, and Jones (1989: 268) cites examples from *Lagamon's Brut*, written in the 1200s. There are also a number of examples in *The Diary of Henry Machin*, written in the 1550s and 1560s (Jones, 1989: 268).

Southern Hemisphere evidence

Modern New Zealand and South African English typically do not have H Dropping. It occurs at a low level of frequency in the speech of some Australians, notably those of Italian ancestry, where interference from Italian might be suspected (Horvath, 1985), and in Falkland Islands English. Tristanian, on the other hand, is characterised not only by the presence of /h/ but also by very extensive H insertion: /h/ occurs very regularly in words which in other varieties begin with a vowel, such as *island, apple, after*. H Dropping is not uncommon on the ONZE Project recordings, but only about 25% of speakers use this feature. This all suggests that

H Dropping was probably much less common in England and Wales in the nineteenth century than it is today. Interestingly, a number of ONZE speakers fall into a category which is absent from modern Britain: they have H Dropping only in the stressed forms of the grammatical words *have, had, has, his, him, her, hers, here.* (Unstressed forms of these words, of course, lack /h/ in all varieties of English and are therefore, as we said above, not to be counted as H Dropping.) H Dropping for them does not occur at all, even variably, in lexical words such as *hammer, hill, house.* One explanation for the presence of this unusual feature in the speech of a sizeable group of our speakers is that it might have been a feature of some forms of nineteenth-century English English which has subsequently disappeared.

British evidence

According to Wells (1982: 255) 'historical details of the spread of H Dropping through England are lacking'. However, there is much that we can deduce about the situation in the mid-nineteenth century, most obviously by noting modern trends and working backwards. Most modern local accents of English and Welsh English currently demonstrate H Dropping. The major exceptions to this are the accents of the English of the northeast and East Anglia although, in keeping with the gradual historical spread of this feature, modern East Anglia is currently acquiring H Dropping: the East Anglian H Retention area is certainly smaller today than it was at the time of the SED fieldwork (see Trudgill, 1986a: 44–6). H Dropping has not yet reached Scotland or Ireland, and indeed Scots (and to a certain extent Scottish English also) preserves /h/ even in final and pre-consonantal position, as in *nicht* = 'night' and *loch.*

In Map 9, we can see the extent of the absence of H Dropping in current English dialects (from Trudgill, 1999). However, in the most conservative of varieties for which we have accurate information, namely the Traditional-dialects investigated by the SED in the 1950s and 1960s, the areas involved are much bigger, as can also be seen from the map. Note too that, at this stage, in addition to the northeastern and East Anglian areas, there is another area in the southwest and a small area in northern Kent which are also characterised by absence of H Dropping, as is the Isle of Wight.

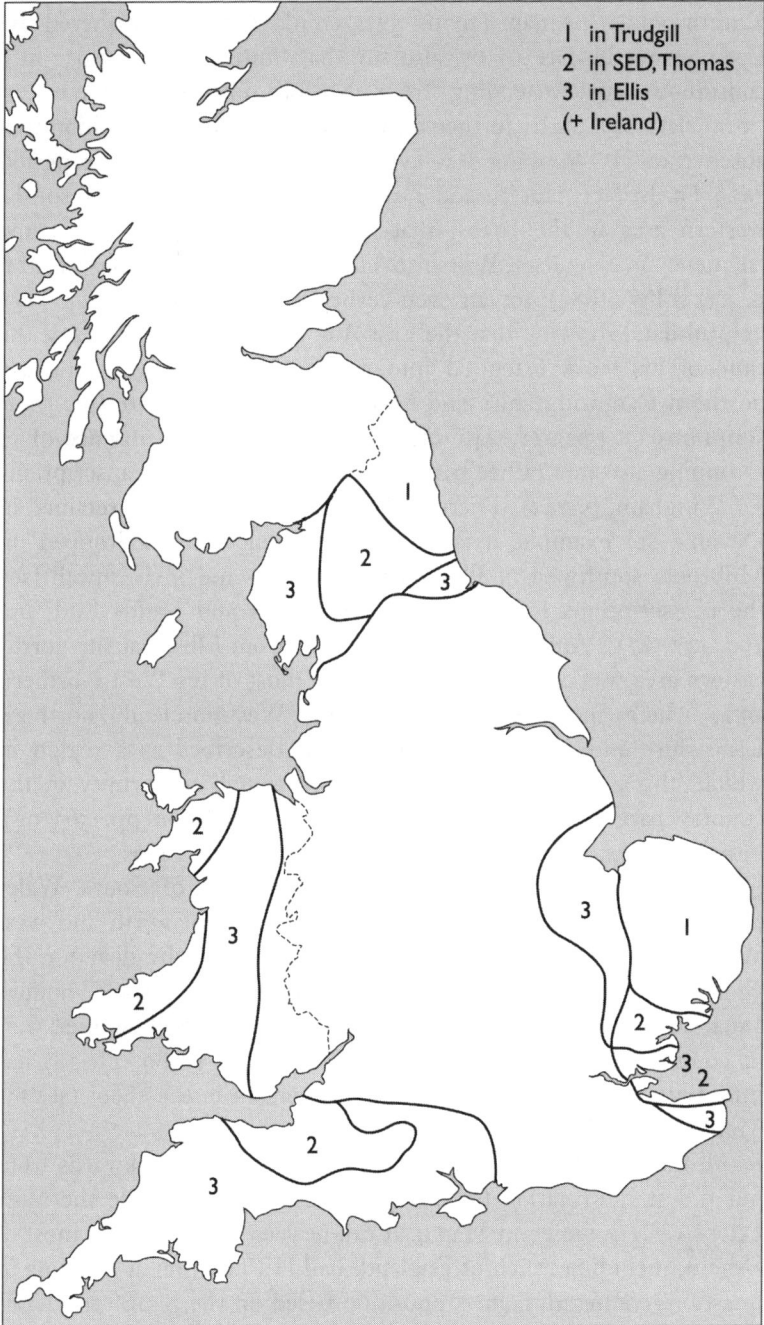

Map 9: /h/-retention

Kurath and Lowman (1970: 32), employing data gathered by Lowman in the late 1930s, also say that 'initial [h] is regular in a continuous area extending from Norfolk into Essex'. We can extrapolate backwards further from this pattern to a supposition that absence of H Dropping was even more widespread in the period 1825–65. In fact, Kurath and Lowman (1970: 32) say, of the south-western area in the 1930s, that 'initial [h] … occurs with some frequency in Somerset–Wiltshire–Hampshire' (see also their map on p. 33). Ellis (1889), for an even earlier period, provides some very helpful data, showing that the East Anglian H Retention area at the time of his work extended into parts of southeast Lincolnshire, northern Cambridgeshire and northern Huntingdonshire (see transcriptions on pp. 211, 249–52, 298, 299). He shows absence of H Dropping also in a rather larger area of Kent (see the transcriptions for Wingham, p. 142). There is also evidence that /h/ is retained in Devon – for example, it is reported as being 'seldom dropped' in Milbrook, southwest of Plymouth (p. 167) – and in Cornwall (see the transcriptions for St Columb, Marazion and Lands End, pp. 169, 172, 173). And there is also evidence from Ellis that the north-eastern area was considerably larger too: most of his West Northern area, which includes south Durham, Westmoreland, northern Lancashire and western Cumberland, is described as a region in which 'the aspirate … is employed with much uniformity in the country part' (p. 542, and see the transcriptions on pp. 563–94). Note that most of Ellis's data was obtained in the 1870s.

H Dropping is found today in the English of South Wales (Wells, 1982: 391). In the Welsh-speaking area of north and west Wales, however, H Dropping does not occur in English for the good reason that /h/ is found in the Welsh of this region (Thomas, 1994: 128 – labelled 2 on the map). The Welsh-speaking area was, of course, larger in 1850 than it is today: Ellis (1889: 13, 14) has information on where the language frontier ran in the 1860s (see his Map of the English Dialect Districts).

All this information now enables us, by working backwards from our oldest information for any given region, to produce the most extensive area shown in Map 9. It can be seen from this that most of Britain, including much of England, had H Retention at the time in question, confirming our supposition based on the Southern Hemisphere evidence. (Ireland still has H Retention to this day.)

In all of the H Dropping areas, this feature is today – and presumably was in 1850 also – variable for many speakers, and is much more common towards the bottom than towards the top of the social scale.

The /hw/–/w/ Merger

The merger of /hw/ and /w/ as in *which/witch* on /w/ is referred to by Wells (1982: 228) as Glide Cluster Reduction. (In varieties which still have this distinction, /hw/ may be [hw], [hʍ] or [ʍ].) Wells suggests that the merger began in lower-class speech in the south of England in early Middle English, became current in educated speech in the 1700s, and was 'usual by 1800'. The merger can be regarded as part of the process of loss of /h/ just described.

Southern Hemisphere evidence

The historical distinction between initial /hw/ and /w/ is widely preserved in New Zealand English (Wells, 1982: 610). Turner (1966: 105) reported that, in 1964, about 50% of first-year students (i.e. people born in about 1946) at Canterbury University, Christchurch, had the distinction. Glide Cluster Reduction is, on the other hand, usual in South African and Australian English. It is possible that the New Zealand pronunciation reflects a greater degree of retention of the distinction in nineteenth-century Britain than suggested by Wells.

British evidence

In support of this, MacMahon says that /hw/ was retained 'by most speakers of educated Southern English until at least the second half of the nineteenth century'. In current regional speech, /hw/ survives totally in Scotland and Ireland (as well as in parts of North America) but has disappeared from all of England except the far north. Map 10 shows the area which had /hw/ according to Ellis, and the rather smaller area in the SED.

Note that a comparison of Maps 9 and 10 reveals a puzzling situation. Accents in the south of England clearly lost /hw/ before they lost /h/: East Anglian dialects have /h/ but not /hw/, for

Map 10: /hw/ retention

instance. It would therefore seem legitimate to assume that there is an implicational scaling effect here due to the relative chronology of the two changes: all speakers who retain /hw/ also retain /h/, while the reverse is not necessarily true. However, there is a small area of northern England, roughly the far northwest of Yorkshire, which Ellis shows as having preserved /hw/ while having lost /h/. The assumption cannot, then, be entirely correct.

/l/

In modern RP and many other forms of English English, /l/ is normally 'clear' before a following vowel or /j/, but 'dark' before a consonant, including /w/, or a pause, regardless of word boundaries. In the non-RP accents of southern England, L Vocalisation is also common; this process affects only dark /l/, and is certainly recent even in London, where it is most advanced today. As Wells points out (1982: 259), there is no reference to it in descriptions of Cockney until the early twentieth century.

Southern Hemisphere evidence

The ONZE data suggests that the clear /l/–dark /l/ allophony of modern England is rather recent. On the ONZE Project recordings 'dark' /l/ is not very 'dark' at all in the speech of most of the informants, and there is little or no L Vocalisation. A number of informants have clear /l/ in all positions. In Tristanian English, too, a clear /l/ is usual after front vowels. In the modern Southern Hemisphere varieties, the pronunciation of /l/ in most or all environments in Australasian English tends to be rather dark, possibly pharyngealised, and the distribution of 'clear' and 'dark' allophonic variants is certainly not as prominent as in many English English accents (Wells, 1982: 603, 609). L Vocalisation is now under way in prepausal and preconsonantal position in New Zealand, but it is obviously a twentieth-century innovation. South African English /l/ is described by Wells (1982: 616) as being 'neutral or clear in quality, without the dark allophones common elsewhere'. Falkland Islands English has the English English type of allophony, with dark /l/ being rather markedly velarised.

British evidence

The British evidence also supports the view that the clear /l/–dark /l/ allophony of English English appears to be a recent addition to English phonology. The SED materials show that, in the Traditional-dialects of the 1950s/60s, dark /l/ was found only south of a line passing between Shropshire and Hereford and proceeding more or less due east to pass between Norfolk and Suffolk. In modern dialects, on the other hand, dark /l/ is now found everywhere except in the northeast (Trudgill, 1999).

L Vocalisation is normal in the SED records only in southeastern Essex, southern Hertfordshire, northwestern Kent, Surrey, Middlesex and Sussex – that is, the areas immediately to the south, east and north of London.

Clear /l/ is usual in all environments in Irish English, except that dark /l/ is 'very common in Belfast (and probably in some country areas to the north and west)' in some phonological environments (Wells, 1982: 446). Clear /l/ is also usual in the Scottish Highlands while, in the Lowlands, dark /l/ is usual in all phonological environments.

T Glottalling

Wells (1982: 261) writes that T Glottalling, the realisation of syllable-final /t/ as [ʔ], 'must have spread very fast in the course of the present century' in British English, and indeed there is plenty of evidence that this is correct.

Southern Hemisphere evidence

Falkland Islands English has T Glottalling, as does Tristanian, although there T Glottalling occurs most often before syllabic /l/ and /n/, as in *button*, *bottle*. None of the other modern Southern Hemisphere Englishes has this feature. It is not surprising, therefore, that there is hardly any glottalling in the speech of the elderly New Zealanders on the ONZE Project recordings, a confirmation, if one were needed, of the relatively recent development of this phenomenon in England.

There is one exception on our tapes to this generalisation – a Mrs German, who was born in 1867 in Clinton and lived in Balclutha, both on the South Island. Her parents were middle-class people who came from Bury St Edmunds, Suffolk. Mrs German preserves a number of obviously East Anglian features in her speech – we discuss these further below. In Mrs German's speech, word-final /t/ is quite often realised as [ʔ]. Although it is often assumed that T Glottalling in England was an urban innovation, it is equally possible that it had its origins in East Anglia: the only area of rural England to have considerable amounts of glottalling in the records of SED is northern East Anglia (see Trudgill, 1974). The fact that Mrs German has this feature suggests that, unlike in the rest of England, it was possibly part of East Anglian English at least from the 1850s. A number of the ONZE Project speakers also have intervocalic /p, t, k/ as [pʔ, tʔ, kʔ]. One such is Mr C. Dixon, who was born in Naseby in 1867 and whose father also came from East Anglia (Norfolk).

British evidence

According to Bailey (1996: 76), observers have been commenting on the phenomenon only since 1860, and early references were almost exclusively to Scotland and to London. The SED records show hardly any instances of T Glottalling except in the London area and northern East Anglia, as just noted. And there is convincing evidence that it reached western areas such as Cardiff (see Mees, 1977) and Liverpool only very recently. In many studies (see, for example, Trudgill, 1988) it has been shown that younger speakers demonstrate more glottalling than older speakers.

Preglottalisation

Preglottalisation (Wells, 1982: 260) is the use of a glottal stop before /p, t, k, tʃ/ in items such as *hopeless* [hoʊʔpləs], *match* [mæʔtʃ]. Preglottalisation of this type is very usual indeed today in very many – perhaps most – English English accents, including RP. As Wells points out, however, it is something which has attracted very little comment from either amateur or professional observers in Britain (although it may be one of the things which leads Americans to describe British accents as 'clipped'). We therefore have no solid information which might lead us to any satisfactory indication of its dating.

Southern Hemisphere evidence

However, when I first started listening to the ONZE tapes, I noticed that there was something about even those speakers who sounded very English that was strange – something which gave their speech a distinctly un-British and/or old-fashioned ring to it, to my ear. I eventually realised what it was: the ONZE speakers show very little evidence of Preglottalisation. Its absence from the New Zealand recordings suggests that Preglottalisation in Britain is a recent and probably late nineteenth-century phenomenon. None of the modern Southern Hemisphere Englishes has Preglottalisation, except for Falkland Islands English and the English of Tristan.

British evidence

Andrésen (1968) dates Preglottalisation to the twentieth century in RP. Interestingly, Andersen (2002) now shows that it is beginning to make an appearance in American English.

CHAPTER 3

New-dialect formation: Stage I – rudimentary levelling and interdialect development

So far, I have argued that colonial Englishes are the result of dialect contact and, specifically, that the Southern Hemisphere Englishes are the result of contact between nineteenth-century varieties of British English. I have also argued that the new-dialect formation that resulted from this dialect contact and subsequent dialect mixture was not a random process. I have maintained that, in tabula rasa situations such as the ones which obtained in New Zealand and Australia and South Africa, it is possible – given sufficient linguistic information about the dialects which contribute to a mixture, and given sufficient demographic information about the proportions of speakers of the different dialects – to make predictions, within certain limitations, about what the outcome of the mixture will be, at least in general terms. Recall that, by 'tabula rasa' situations, I mean those in which there is no prior-existing population speaking the language in question, either in the location in question or nearby. Recall, too, that this deterministic view of new-dialect formation entails that similarities between different geographical varieties of a single language may be due, not to any direct contact between them, but to the fact that they have resulted from mixtures of similar dialects in similar proportions at similar times. I am here, as indicated earlier, thinking in particular of the similarities between Falkland Islands, South African and, especially, Australian and New Zealand English. In this and the following two chapters, I now go on to examine the new-dialect formation process in more detail.

NEW-DIALECT FORMATION

In earlier work on new-dialect formation (Trudgill, 1986a), I suggested that certain sorts of sociolinguistic situation involving contact between mutually intelligible dialects – colonial situations, new towns, rapid urbanisation – can lead to the development of new dialects. After examining a number of case studies, I arrived at a description of the mechanisms involved in new-dialect formation. As a result of further work based on an analysis of the ONZE Project Corpus, I now argue that new-dialect formation consists of six key processes.

1. Mixing

This is, rather obviously, the coming together in a particular location of speakers of different dialects of the same language, or of readily mutually intelligible languages. For example, as we saw in Chapter 1, Penny is very clear about the role of dialect mixing in the formation of colonial dialects of South American Spanish. He points out, in an echo of comments above about American and Australian English, that 'the degree of geographical variation in American Spanish is considerably less than the variation observable within Peninsula Spanish' (2000: 137), and he ascribes this to 'the mixing of mutually comprehensible dialects implicit in the colonization process' (p. 138). Moreover, 'the distribution of features in American Spanish can often be reasonably sought in the processes of immigration from Spain and the patterns of dialect mixing which sprang from these processes'. He points out that, while many American Spanish features such as *yeismo* (the merger of /j/ and /ʎ/) appear to be southern in origin, there are also a number of features, such as the affrication of /tr/ (p. 157), which are clearly from northern Spain.

2. Levelling

This involves the loss of demographically minority variants. In a dialect mixture situation such as that present in a newly settled colony, large numbers of variants from the different dialects involved in the mixture will abound. As time passes, the variants present in the mixture will begin to be subject to reduction. The point is, however, that this reduction will not take place in a haphazard manner, or as a result of social factors such as status. In determining who accommodates to who – and therefore which forms are retained and which lost – demographic factors involving proportions of different dialect speakers present will be vital. It should be understood that this is not a matter of one dialect supplanting all other dialects, but of a particular dialect variant of an individual feature supplanting all other variants. Penny (2000: 156, 157) acknowledges the demography inherent in this process when he ascribes the prevalence of word-final /n/ as [ŋ] in South American Spanish both to the fact that this form is prevalent in Andalusia *and* to the fact that 'it has its origins ... also in [the dialects] from the northwest of the Peninsula, where this feature is to be heard, still today, in Galician, Asturian, Leonese, and Cantabrian varieties'. Lipski (1994: 46) agrees, and says that 'the "Andalusian" traits of American Spanish are, in their great majority, common to both Andalusian and Castilian'. Morin (1994: 206), too, in his discussion of the growth of Quebec French, talks of the importance of 'demographic weight'; and Juneau (1972: 275) says that 'the features which disappeared [from Quebec French] are generally those which were characteristic of a restricted Gallo-Roman dialect area, those which survived belonged, on the contrary, to larger dialect areas'; while Flikeid (1994: 319) describes, for Acadian French, 'the abandonment of traits which were marked because they were too localised and not shared' (my translations).

3. Unmarking

The reduction of variants over time is also not haphazard from the point of view of purely linguistic forces. Degrees of linguistic markedness and regularity or simplicity may be involved, such that unmarked and more regular forms may survive even if they are not majority forms. Unmarking can be regarded as a subtype of levelling. Moag (1977) showed that, in the development of Fiji Hindi through dialect mixture, the main contributing dialects were Standard Hindi, Bhojpuri and Awadi. Normally in Fiji Hindi, the form which has survived is the one which is favoured by two out of the three contributing dialects (Trudgill, 1986a: 102). However, note what

happens where there is no such two-to-one majority, as in the case
of the optative first-person plural ending on verbs:

Std. Hindi	Bhojpuri	Awadi	>	Fiji Hindi
-ẽ:	-ĩ:	-i:		-i:

Here, in a three-way competition, the non-nasal ending survives at
the expense of forms with (phonologically marked) nasal vowels.
Similarly, Penny (2000: 142) points out that American Spanish
seems to derive more features from the southern Iberian dialects of
Andalusia than from other areas, but that this may be in part
because these are features which 'offer greatest structural
simplicity'. These include, amongst others, the mergers of /θ/ and
/s/; of /ʎ/ and /j/; and of syllable-final /r/ and /l/. I would also
point out that it is notable that the complex eastern Andalusian
eight-vowel system and its concomitant patterns of vowel harmony
(Hernandez-Campoy and Trudgill, 2003) did not make it into
American Spanish.

4. Interdialect development

Interdialect forms can be defined as forms which were not actually
present in any of the dialects contributing to the mixture, but which
arise out of interaction between them. Such forms are of three
types:

a) They may be forms which are simpler or more regular than any
of the forms present in the original dialect mixture.
b) Interdialect forms may also be intermediate forms. In Trudgill
(1986a), I suggested that these are most usually forms which are
phonetically intermediate between two contributing forms in the
mixture. Penny (2000: 41), however, says that:

> there seems no reason to limit interdialectalism to the
> phonological domain, and therefore it seems we should expect
> dialect mixing to produce, say, morphological or syntactical
> variants which are novel and intermediate between those
> that existed before the mixture came into being.

He gives a good illustration of this (pp. 90–3) from Spanish pronominal clitics. Trudgill (1986a), too, gives some morphosyntactic examples. Here we should also note, however, that interdialect is not the only source of intermediate forms. Samuels (1972: 108) has pointed out that forms entering into a dialect mixture which happen to be intermediate between other contributing forms may be more likely to survive, even if they are in a minority, simply as a result of their linguistically intermediate status. He shows that the colonial English of fourteenth-century and fifteenth-century Ireland was the result of a mixture – an 'amalgam', as he puts it – of regional English forms derived in the main from Herefordshire, Gloucestershire, Somerset, Devon, Shropshire, Cheshire and Lancashire. He shows that at least one clearly minority form, *euch* 'each', originally from southern Hereford, was the form to survive in Anglo-Irish because it was 'a convenient compromise' between the northern *uch* of Lancashire and Cheshire and the southern *ech* of Gloucestershire, Somerset and Devon. The determinism-in-new-dialect-formation argument, that I am pursuing in this book leads me to suggest that this kind of compromise development will in fact only occur when the surviving intermediate form is linguistically intermediate between two (or more) majority variants of roughly equivalent demographic strength.

c) Interdialect forms may also be forms which are the result of hyperadaptation. The best-known form of this is 'hypercorrection', in which speakers attempt to use forms from higher status accents, but employ an incorrect analysis and extend changes to items where they are inappropriate (see Samuels, 1972: 106). That this can have permanent consequences for colonial varieties is shown by the fact that in many forms of Jamaican English (Cassidy and Le Page, 1980), as well as in Tristanian (see above), all stressed-vowel-initial words can actually begin with /h/.

5. Reallocation

Occasionally, even after levelling, more than one competing variant left over from the original mixture may survive. Where this happens, reallocation will occur, such that variants originally from different regional dialects will in the new dialect become social class variants, stylistic variants or, in the case of phonology, allophonic variants (see Trudgill, 1986a; Britain and Trudgill, 1999). I have argued, for instance, that 'Canadian Raising', which has resulted in the distinctive and markedly different allophones of the PRICE and MOUTH vowels, i.e. [əɪ, əʊ], before voiceless consonants, is the result of reallocation. The argument is, briefly, that in the colonial dialect mixture situation that preceded the formation of Canadian English, there were variants of these diphthongs both with central onsets – from Scotland, for example – and variants with more open onsets – perhaps from southern England. In the levelling process, both types of variant survived but were reallocated allophonic status. The diphthongs with central onsets, requiring less tongue movement for their articulation, were allocated to phonological environments producing short vocalic variants in English, i.e. before voiceless consonants, while the wider diphthongs, requiring more tongue movement, were allocated to the environments producing longer vowels, i.e. before voiced consonants or a word boundary. This thesis is strengthened by the fact that 'Canadian Raising' is also found in a number of other colonial varieties. Indeed, it occurs 'in *nearly every* form of non-creolised, mixed, colonial English outside Australasia and South Africa' (Trudgill, 1986: 160), including the Englishes of White Bahamians, White Bermudans and St Helena (Trudgill, 1986), and of Charleston, South Carolina (Kurath and McDavid, 1961) – as well as in the mixed dialects of the relatively recently settled English Fens (Britain, 1997). Falkland Islands English, as we noted earlier, also has 'Canadian Raising': MOUTH is generally a 'fast' diphthong [œʉ ~ ɜʉ] before voiceless consonants, as in *south*, but a 'slow' diphthong [æˑʊ ~ aˑʊ] elsewhere (for the terms 'fast' and 'slow' diphthong, see Kurath, 1964: 153). Similarly, PRICE is [ɐɪ ~ ɜɪ] before voiceless consonants, but [ɑˑɪ] elsewhere. Tristanian English has 'Canadian raising' only of PRICE, with the two variants being [ɐɪ] and [ɒˑɛ].

6. Focussing

Focussing (see Le Page and Tabouret-Keller, 1985) is the process by means of which the new variety acquires norms and stability. Focussing is not to be indentified with levelling. Although focussing implies levelling, the reverse is not the case: a reduction in the number of variants does not in itself lead to stability and societally shared norms. Processes 1–5 can collectively be referred to as *koinéisation*. Koinéisation plus focussing (process 6) constitute *new-dialect formation*. As argued for at length in Trudgill (1986a), a key microsociolinguistic mechanism involved in new-dialect formation is accommodation between speakers in face-to-face interaction. As we saw in Chapter 1, accommodation appears to be the result of a biologically inherited tendency for human beings to behave like the other human beings that they associate with. We shall examine the extent to which accommodation does and does not operate at different stages of the new-dialect formation process below.

We can distinguish between three different chronological stages in the new-dialect formation process which also roughly correspond to three successive generations of speakers. I now proceed, in the rest of this chapter and in Chapters 4 and 5, to examine the distribution of processes 1–6 over these three stages, as revealed by an analysis of the development of New Zealand English on the basis of the ONZE Corpus material.

STAGE I

Rudimentary levelling

The first stage involves the initial contact and mixing between adult speakers of different regional and social varieties at assembly points in the British Isles, on the long boat journey out, and early on in the new location. In these situations, certain limited types of accommodation by adult speakers to one another in face-to-face interaction – bearing in mind that adults are generally only capable of limited amounts of accommodation – would have occurred. As a consequence, rudimentary dialect levelling would have taken place, most notably of minority, very localised Traditional-dialect features. It is also possible that comprehensibility played a role here: any very localised features which diminished mutual intelligibility would have been particularly susceptible to loss.

This factor would have been an even more important factor in earlier centuries, such as during the settlement of America, when Traditional-dialects would have been more prevalent, and more different from one another. For Canadian French, Mougeon and Beniak (1994: 2) specifically cite the role of difficulties of comprehension between speakers of different seventeen-century French patois, even given that nearly all of the colonists came from the northern *langue d'oïl* area, in leading to levelling.

Work on Canadian French has also suggested another reason why Traditional-dialects may have played a smaller role than might have been expected in the mixture. The greater linguistic distance between such dialects and General English (Wells, 1982: 2) opens up the possibility of bidialectalism, dialect switching, and the maintenance of the two systems as separate rather than constituting points on a continuum – for example, most Swiss Germans and many Lowland Scots today are bidialectal in a way that is not open to speakers from central Germany or southern England. Barbaud (1994: 83) cites Lortie (1914) as suggesting that 32% of the seventeenth-century French Canadian colonists were bidialectal/bilingual in their local patois and some form of French, and that in the new colonial situation in Canada they would, simply in order to be intelligible to others, have switched to French and abandoned their patois.

The importance of the sea journey to the new colony should also not be underestimated – the voyage to New Zealand did last from four to six months. Turner (1994: 278) asserts that levelling could have taken place 'at sea' in the case of Australian English. And Penny (2000: 142) points out, with reference to colonial Spanish, that 'the voyage to the Caribbean took several months'. According to Chaudenson (1994: 172), seventeenth-century francophone colonists on their way to Canada or New Caledonia could spend weeks or even months waiting in ports on the French coast, and maybe even as long as a year on the journey. (This also may have meant that the dialects of the port cities themselves could have played a significant role. For example, Hull (1994: 191) ascribes the well-known affrication in Quebec French of /t, d/ > /ts, dz/ before high front vowels, e.g. *tu* 'you' [tsy], to the presence of this same feature in the seventeenth-century dialect of the western French port city of Nantes.)

That rudimentary dialect levelling of such features occurred in or on the way to New Zealand can be inferred indirectly but very readily from the ONZE Project data. There are very many features of nineteenth-century British Isles Traditional-dialects which are not even vestigially present in the ONZE Corpus data. This is also, of course, true of modern New Zealand English, as well as of South African English and Australian English. A significant number of emigrants were agricultural workers (see Belich, 1996) who would, for the most part, have been rural Traditional-dialect speakers, so we have to suppose that such features did at least make it on to the boat. We therefore have to assume that these features were levelled out very early on because of their extreme minority status.

One nineteenth-century British feature whose almost total absence from the ONZE Project recordings can be ascribed to rudimentary levelling is the merger of /v/ and /w/ as /w/, giving *village* as *willage*, which was a (recessive) feature of many south-of-England dialects at this time (see Trudgill et al., 2003). This did make it into a number of other colonial varieties, such as those of Tristan da Cunha (see Schreier, 2003) and the Bahamas, perhaps because of the earlier date of formation of these varieties – the feature would have been more widespread in the late eighteenth and early nineteenth century than in the mid-nineteenth century.

One interesting and valuable indication of the nature of rudimentary levelling can be obtained by comparing the speech of the core ONZE Project informants with that of speakers who were excluded from the main analyses because they were not born in New Zealand. One such excluded speaker, Mrs Susan McFarlane, is of particular interest. She was born about 1845 and, as far as we can tell from the content of her recording, she grew up in Friockheim, Angus, Scotland. She came to New Zealand in 1878 when she was in her thirties. She was recorded in Dunedin, aged 102. We know that Mrs McFarlane did not go to school; that her father was a gamekeeper; that she worked in service; and that her husband was a prison warder in Perth, Scotland, before emigrating to New Zealand. (We also know that she met Queen Victoria – 'a dear little woman'.) Her speech is remarkable as a record of mid-nineteenth-century Scottish English.

It is true that Mrs McFarlane shares many phonological features with those of the ONZE core speakers who have Scottish elements in their speech (see Chapter 2). For example, she is one of a number of speakers on the ONZE tapes who demonstrate Aitken's Law (Aitken, 1984: 94). Mrs McFarlane also preserves as distinct the KIT vowel in *first*, the STRUT vowel in *fur* and the DRESS vowel in *fern*, as some of the core informants do. She also has a vowel system that resembles the basic Scottish English system, in which the vowels of FOOT and GOOSE, TRAP and PALM, and LOT and THOUGHT are not distinct, and which is also found in the speech of a number of core informants.

On the other hand, she also has, albeit spasmodically and unsystematically, a number of other Scottish features which differ dramatically from those found in the speech of any of our New Zealand-born informants. In analysing these linguistic characteristics, we have to make a distinction between Scottish English, on the one hand, and the Traditional-dialect Scots (see Chapter 2), on the other. Although Mrs McFarlane has a vowel system which is not unlike that of our other 'Scottish' speakers, her distribution of lexical items over these Scottish English vowels is sometimes very typical of Scots: she not infrequently uses forms such as *oot, doon, hoose, aboot,* etc.; *airm* 'arm'; *canna* 'can't'; *nae* 'no'; *craw* 'crow'; *mither* 'mother'. She also often has the TRAP vowel in items such as *watch, wash, what, warder, all*. And many of her LOT words actually have the vowel of GOAT, a typical Midland Scottish dialect feature (see Grant and Dixon, 1921: 50; Aitken, 1984: 100). Her KIT vowel is sometimes also very central, unlike all the other ONZE informants with Scottish-type vowel systems. Mrs McFarlane also has /x/, not just in place names, surnames or the exclamation *och!*, like some of the ONZE core informants, but also in items such as /roxt/ 'wrought = worked' (Aitken, 1984: 101). And she has occasional instances of initial /f/ in items such as *when* (Aitken, 1984: 102). Her /r/ is most frequently an alveolar flap but she also employs a trilled [r] and not infrequently a uvular [ʁ] (see Aitken, 1984: 102). And, in her pronominal system, she uses *hit* 'it' and *wur* 'our' (see Grant and Dixon, 1921: 95–8).

The point is, then, that Mrs McFarlane has many dialectal Scots features in her speech that do not occur in the speech of any of the ONZE core informants. I suggest that such features would also have been present in the speech of many other emigrants from Scotland to New Zealand, and that the absence of such dialectal features from the English of the children of these emigrants – that is, the first English-speaking children born in New Zealand (for example, the Mobile Unit informants) – is precisely the result of a rudimentary levelling process which led to the gradual diminution in use of most Traditional-dialect features at the first stage and their consequent absence from the ONZE Project tapes.

We can suppose that this was because such forms would have been, *looked at individually*, very much in a minority. That is, large numbers of speakers of Traditional-dialects emigrated to New Zealand but, since many individual Traditional-dialect features are found only in rather small geographical areas – hence the observation that such dialects change every few miles or so (see Chapter 1) – there would have been a tendency for such individual features to be found in the speech of only very few immigrants. For example, it is highly probable that, in 1840, every single agricultural worker in northeastern Norfolk would have had the phonological characteristic of lowering the DRESS vowel to TRAP before front voiced fricatives, as in *never, together* (see Trudgill, 2003). However, since this feature was confined to a very small area of England, the number of people on any boat and in any new settlement in New Zealand with this feature would have been extremely small, and it would quite readily have become even more infrequent in the dialect mixture as a result of this small minority of speakers accommodating, albeit no doubt spasmodically and unsystematically as Mrs McFarlane has done, to the overwhelming majority.

In Trudgill (1986a), I argued that which features speakers accommodate to in the speech of others can be accounted for by *salience*. In general, it is salient features – those which are 'noticed' (cf. Schmidt, 1990) by speakers – which are accommodated to. I shall argue below that, in fact, salience is not relevant at most stages of the new-dialect formation process. However, this does not apply to rudimentary levelling, where accommodation would have operated in the normal way amongst adults, and salience could have been a factor.

Normative attitudes which had been developed in Britain, e.g. negative sentiments towards rural speech, may also have been relevant at this stage amongst these adults, and might well have played a part in this process. (In Chapter 7, I argue for the irrelevance of normative attitudes at later stages in the new-dialect formation process, but not at Stage I.)

Interdialect development

Accommodation at the first stage of new-dialect formation may also lead to the occurrence of another of the key new-dialect formation processes, namely the development of interdialect forms. As we have seen, these can be defined as forms which were not actually present in any of the dialects contributing to the mixture, but which arise out of interaction between them. It emerges, however, that, unlike in new-town koinés and other similar forms of dialect contact, interdialect plays a relatively unimportant role in tabula rasa colonial new-dialect formation scenarios. This is because inter-dialect forms are most usually generated by partial accommodation and/or misanalyses on the part of adult speakers. Given, as we saw in Chapter 1, that most of the work of new-dialect formation of the tabula rasa colonial type is carried out by children at Stages II and III, interdialect forms arise for the most part only at Stage I, where mixing and accommodation by adults do play a role.

Nevertheless, some possible candidates for the status of interdialect forms can be discerned in new colonial dialects. We saw that interdialect forms are of three types: intermediate forms, which result from partial accommodation; simpler or more regular forms; and hyperadaptative forms – the latter two resulting from mis-analysis or reanalysis during accommodation.

For intermediate forms, Mougeon and Beniak (1994: 26) mention for Canadian French 'innovations such as intermediate compromise forms' (my translation). They cite (p. 40) an example originally provided by Rivard (1914: 59): three different French forms of *gens* 'people', Standard /ʒã/, Picard /ʒẽ/ and Saintongeais /hã/, have combined to produce Québécois /hẽ/.

As far as more regular forms are concerned, we can note the Afrikaans verb system as discussed by Combrink (1978). Combrink compares the present-tense inflectional endings of Standard Dutch and Afrikaans:

'to work'

	Dutch		Afrikaans	
	singular	*plural*	*singular*	*plural*
1.	werk	werken	werk	werk
2.	werkt	werken/werkt	werk	werk
3	werkt	werken	werk	werk

Combrink shows that, in the Dutch dialects that were taken to the Cape from the seventeenth century onwards, there were twenty-three different systems of present-tense indicative verb morphology. In North Holland, South Holland, and Utrecht alone there were five (shown here for the singular only):

	A	B	C	D	E
1.	-	-t	-	-	-
2.	-	-t	-t	-	-e
3.	-	-t	-t	-t	-t

He says (p. 75):

imagine the amount of noise via inflections versus the amount of communication via stems, if 73% of the Dutch Cape settlers used five of these systems and the other 27% something like eighteen other systems!

and he ascribes this development in colonial Dutch (later Afrikaans) to 'interdialectal noise deletion'.

It is, however, equally possible that this simplification in Afrikaans is the result, instead or as well, of language contact.

For hyperadaptive forms, a common interdialectal feature on the ONZE tapes is hyperadaptive – in fact, hypercorrect – initial /h/ in, for example, *and*, *I*, *apple*. About one in ten of the informants have some instances of this feature. As we have seen, /h/-insertion is also the norm in Tristan da Cunha and some forms of Jamaican, presumably for the same reason. One of the ONZE informants, Mrs McKeany, who was born in 1866 in Cambridge, North Island, and whose father came from Ireland, is extraordinary in this respect and demonstrates behaviour I have not come across before from any other English speaker: nearly all stressed-vowel-initial words in her speech begin with /h/; even more unusually, nearly all words which begin with /w/ actually begin with /ʍ/ in her idiolect. Other speakers make such hyperadaptations only variably. This phenomenon is not totally unknown in England, of course, but my suggestion is that the very high level of occurrence of this phenomenon in the speech of these ONZE speakers indicates that they inherited such hyperadaptations from the speech of people of their parents' generation, amongst whom it was unusually widespread as a result of misanalyses during the course of accommodation. It is important, however, that this interdialect form did not survive into Stage III in New Zealand English.

I also suggest that the origins of the close TRAP vowel in New Zealand English may lie not only in the importation of such realisations directly from England (see also Chapter 2), but also in interdialect development. Anglicised (or, in the words of the late David Abercrombie, 'anglophile') Scottish accents of the type known in Edinburgh as 'Morningside' and in Glasgow as 'Kelvinside', after the upper-middle-class suburbs with which they are associated, can have [ɛ] in the lexical set of TRAP – as Wells points out, 'unlike most Scots who have [a – ɑ]' (1982: 403). Wells even suggests that, in these accents, /ɛ/ and /æ/ may be merged before or after velar consonants so that, for example, *kettle* and *cattle* are homophonous. Grant (1913: 51–2) also writes of [æ] that

> its use by some [Scottish] speakers instead of [a] ... is probably an importation from Southern English. It is heard most frequently about Edinburgh and Glasgow. Most Scottish speakers who attempt to pronounce [mæn] say [mɛn] which is the Cockney pronunciation and to be avoided.

A number of ONZE informants combine unmistakably Scottish accents with an /æ/ which is realised as [ɛ] in a very 'Morningside' manner. I do not necessarily claim, however, that this feature was imported to New Zealand from Edinburgh or Glasgow, although in some cases it might have been in spite of the fact that most emigrants were not from the upper middle class. I suggest rather that a particular interdialect mechanism may have been at work in the New Zealand context – and that this mechanism was identical to the one which gave rise to the 'Morningside' pronunciation in the first place.

The clue to what this mechanism might have been comes once again from the speech of Mrs McFarlane. As we just saw, she was not born in New Zealand and is therefore not one of the core ONZE Project informants. However, her behaviour as a Scottish adult accommodating to the speech of non-Scots in the New Zealand context can give us an indication of the sorts of processes that may have occurred in the speech of our informants' parents as they accommodated to each other – processes which are, of course, otherwise lost to us.

To explain why Mrs McFarlane's treatment of the TRAP vowel is significant, we first have to look at what happens to her FACE vowel. (Wells's system of keywords representing lexical sets does not really work for Scots, since these dialects are radically different in their vowel systems and distribution of vowels over lexical items from all other varieties of English – as we shall see below, Johnston (1997a) uses a different set of keywords for Scots – but we shall continue in what follows to use Wells's system where this does not cause confusion.) Mrs McFarlane's normal vowel in the lexical set of FACE is, as was and is usual in Scotland, monophthongal [e]. There are also, however, some surprisingly extreme diphthongal tokens of FACE on her recordings. What appears to have happened to bring about this development is very interesting, and can be interpreted according to the phonetic clues as follows.

Many Scots dialects, though not Scottish English, have two contrastive vowels corresponding to the single PRICE vowel of other varieties. The first of these can be written /ae/ and occurs in Aitken's Law long environments (see Chapter 2), as in *fire, size, live, tied, pie*; Johnston (1997a) refers to this lexical set in Scots as the TRY class. The other can be written /ʌi/ and occurs in Aitken's Law short environments, as in *night, time, tide*; Johnston refers to this lexical set as the BITE class. These two vowels have to be considered contrastive in many dialects of Scots because of the pronunciation of items such as *pay*. A number of varieties of Scots (see Mather and Speitel, 1975) – including even, for example, lower-class Edinburgh speech – employ a vowel in the lexical set of *pay, way, stay* which is distinct from the /e/ of *face*, etc. (see Grant and Dixon, 1921: 57; Aitken, 1984: 95). This is because they have retained the Middle Scots (and Middle English) distinction between the vowels of the sets of *made, face* and *maid, pay*, originally /a:/ versus /ai/. In these dialects the vowel of *pay*, etc. is a diphthong of the type [ʌi ~ ʌi] which is identical with the BITE vowel and, crucially, distinct from the TRY vowel, such that *pay* and *pie* are not homophonous. Johnston (1997a: 463) lists English FACE words which have /ʌi/ in Scots as including *ay, may, pay, gey, hay, clay, stay; change, chain; baillie, tailor, gaol.*

Scottish English		Scots		
/e/	/ai/	/e/	/ʌi /	/ae/
face, pay	price [ʌi]	face	price	pie
	pie [ae]		pay	

One reasonable conjecture here is that Mrs McFarlane, under the influence of speakers of New Zealand English and/or English English, has, from time to time, accommodated phonologically rather than phonetically to the diphthongs present in their speech by extending this BITE/*pay* vowel, which is already present in her phonemic inventory, to a whole group of words from the FACE set – FACE and *pay* having the same vowel in most forms of English – in which she originally did not and most often still does not have it. Her pronunciation of *pay* was already similar to that of modern New Zealand English, and once in New Zealand she spasmodically extended this pronunciation to the rest of the words in the English FACE set. This type of accommodation resembles the strategy labelled 'merger by transfer', as outlined in Trudgill and Foxcroft (1978) and Labov (1994), in which two vowels are merged phonologically rather than phonetically by the gradual transfer of lexical items from one vowel to another until all such items have been transferred, and the vowel in question therefore disappears.

We can employ the same interpretation in examining Mrs McFarlane's vowel in the lexical set of TRAP. This is not infrequently a dramatically close [ɛ] or something approaching this. This is rather remarkable since, in nearly all forms of Scots and Scottish English, as we have noted before, the vowel in this set is a low vowel of the type [a ~ ʌ ~ ɑ], and she herself also very often uses a vowel of this quality. A reasonable conjecture, once again, therefore, is that Mrs McFarlane has adopted a similar strategy in this case also. That is, under the influence of speakers who have a vowel in this lexical set with the phonetic quality [ɛ ~ æ], which is radically different from her own – people with southeast of England-type accents, for example – she has replaced it with the vowel from her own phonemic inventory which is closest to theirs, namely her DRESS vowel. (I do not include here her pronunciations of words such as *grass*, *after*, *marriage*, which are pronounced with the DRESS vowel in very many Scottish dialects (see Grant and Dixon, 1921: 44), although these may also have provided some of the input into the modern New Zealand English close TRAP vowel.)

I suggest, therefore, that Mrs McFarlane is using an accommodation strategy of a type which appears to be totally absent from the speech of our core informants who, as children, would have been more successful at mastering phonetic detail, and at correctly analysing the structure of phonological systems, than someone who, like her, arrived as an adult. Crucially, this sort of phonological, as opposed to phonetic, accommodation may have played a role in reinforcing the development of the close realisation of TRAP in New Zealand English – not by leading the way in the gradual phonetic raising of TRAP over time, but in the total phonological *replacement* of the TRAP vowel, at least in some lexical items, by the DRESS vowel as an interdialect phenomenon.

CHAPTER 4

Stage II – variability and apparent levelling in new-dialect formation

It is at the second stage of the new-dialect formation process that the unique ONZE Project Corpus comes into its own. Most of the work on new-dialect formation which is discussed in Trudgill (1986a), and indeed most studies in this field generally, have focussed either on microsociolinguistic individual accommodation events in face-to-face interaction, in the *first* stage of the process (see Giles, 1973; Trudgill, 1982), or on macrosociolinguistic society-wide processes in the *third*, new-dialect formation-through-focussing stage (see, for example, Omdal, 1977). We are, however, not very well provided at all with descriptions of this *second* stage. This is hardly surprising. It is much easier to report on what has happened during the course of new-dialect formation *after* the event, when the new dialect is in place and is readily susceptible to linguistic description, than during the relatively chaotic period while it is actually happening, and when there is in any case no guarantee that there will actually be a new-dialect outcome at all (see Maehlum, 1992; Kerswill, 1994). Here, however, I am fortunately, and very unusually, able to report on the development of a new contact-induced dialect of English where both the fact and the detailed nature of the outcome are actually known. This is due to the remarkable evidence provided by the ONZE Corpus concerning the second stage of new-dialect formation. This evidence, resulting from an analysis of real data taken from the second stage of such a development while it was actually in progress, will enable us to enlarge on and refine the largely speculative thinking about the second stage of new-dialect formation which was developed deductively in Trudgill (1986a). As we shall see, the role of children was crucial at this second stage. At Stage I, adults clearly played an important part in effecting the various forms of accommodation that went on both on the boat and after arrival in the new colony. At Stage II, however, it is children who are vital because they are the ones who are forced to react to the plethora of dialect forms with which they are surrounded, in the speech of adults, in the development of their own individual varieties.

EXTREME VARIABILITY

This second stage of the process, for which the ONZE Corpus provides direct rather than inferred evidence, is characterised by considerable variability, because of the mixing that occurred in the previous generation, as considered in Chapter 3. In the second generation, children, having many different linguistic models to aim at and with no particular reason to select one over another, demonstrate considerable inter-individual *and* intra-individual variability.

Of course, the conventional sociolinguistic wisdom is that children speak like their peers rather than, for example, like their parents or teachers. The evidence for this is overwhelming, as we noted earlier. However, as we also noted earlier, there are certain unusual situations where children are unable to accommodate to the peer-group dialect because there is no common peer-group dialect for them to accommodate to. As we saw in our discussion of colonial lag, Berthele (2000) showed that children at a private school in Switzerland adopt individual accommodation strategies because there is no single peer-group dialect for them to acquire. The same must have been true in early New Zealand. Unlike in stable situations where children normally acquire the dialect of their peers, in diffuse dialect-contact situations the role of adults will be more significant than is usually the case.

The complicated role played by the models provided by adults can be illustrated through the example of one particularly interesting ONZE Corpus speaker, Mrs German, who was mentioned earlier. Her parents, it will be recalled, came from Suffolk. Mrs

German preserves a number of East Anglian features in her speech which were almost certainly acquired from her parents. Her phonology does not, at a first listening, seem particularly East Anglian. It is, however, entirely compatible with her having acquired some of the East Anglian phonology of her parents. For example, she has /ʌ/ rather than /ʊ/ in STRUT, and /a:/rather than /æ/ in BATH, and is therefore clearly speaking a form of southern as opposed to northern English English. Moreover, unusually on these recordings (see Chapter 6), she is almost entirely non-rhotic. This therefore places her, as it were, in the southeast rather than the southwest of England. She also has none of the features stereotypically associated with the Home Counties and London – which leaves us, by default, with an origin in East Anglia.

There are, moreover, a number of features which, at a closer listening, are certainly due to her acquisition of some aspects of the English of her East Anglian parents, even if these do not tally with East Anglian English in all details:

1. The word *was* is pronounced /wʊz/ rather than /wɒz/. This is now somewhat archaic, even in northern rural East Anglia, and it is interesting to find that it may have been general, even in middle-class East Anglian speech, during the nineteenth century.

2. Alone of all our speakers, Mrs German pronounces the words *home* and *homestead* with the FOOT vowel /ʊ/ rather than /ou/. Mrs German's pronunciation of these two words represents the vestiges of a feature which is well known to English dialectologists – the 'East Anglian short o'. In closed syllables, items descended from Middle English /o:/, but not from ME /ou/, are shortened to /ʊ/ so that, for example, *road* rhymes with *good* (Trudgill, 1974).

3. Mrs German also consistently has distinct vowels in *snow* as opposed to *no*, and in *place* as opposed to *play*, reflecting the different origins these vowels have in Middle English (see Chapter 2). The speech of Norfolk – but not Suffolk – to this day preserves the vowels of *no* and *snow* as distinct, as /u:/ versus /ʌu/; while *place* and *play* were until quite recently distinguished as /e:/ versus /æi/. Mrs German has /ou/ versus /ɔu/; and /ei/ versus /ɛi/ for these sets.

4. The vowel of NURSE is a short [ɜ] rather than a long [ɜ:]. It has

been shown (Trudgill, 1997) that earlier forms of northern East Anglian English had seven short, checked vowels rather than six. The additional vowel (see Chapter 6) occurred in the lexical set of *church*, *work*, *first* (but not *earth*) and was phonetically [ɐ]. Mrs German's accent seems to suggest that southern forms of East Anglian English also had this vowel, in that she has an apparently partially dedialectalised vowel with the newer London-based closer quality, but the older East Anglian lack of length.

At least one feature in her phonology, however, is most definitely not East Anglian or even English English in origin – the vowels of LOT and CAUGHT are not distinct in her speech, so that *daughter* rhymes with *hotter*. The most likely explanation is that this is a Scottish English feature which she acquired from the very large number of speakers of Scottish or Scottish-influenced varieties of English present in her local community – Scottish emigration to the area where she lived in New Zealand was particularly heavy.

This complexity is typical of the sort of dialect-mixture situation Mrs German grew up in. I suggest that children at the second stage of new-dialect formation have considerable freedom to select variants from different dialects – spoken not only by their parents but also by everyone else in the community – and form them into new combinations, such as Mrs German's mixture of East Anglian and Scottish vowel systems.

This appearance of new combinations of features is one of three main types of linguistic variability which are to be found at the second stage of the new-dialect formation process as illustrated by the ONZE archive. I now discuss these in turn.

Original combinations

As we have just noted, at this second stage of new-dialect formation, as a result of there being no pressure from a peer-group to conform and many different adult models to follow, children have considerable freedom during language acquisition to select variants from different dialects at will. (I also see a role here for patterns of interaction, but I will discuss this further in Chapter 7.) Earlier hypothetical work (Trudgill, 1986a) suggested that this would mean that children at the second stage would be free to combine features from different dialects which are present in a contact situation into new and hitherto nonexistent combinations. This is, of course, the reason why new dialects consist, in part, of precisely such new combinations – though, at this second stage, these new combinations are likely to be many and individual rather than unique and society-wide.

As indicated by the case of Mrs German, this process is clearly exemplified in the ONZE Project data. There are a large number of instances of such individual combinations, particularly in the case of speakers born in the twenty years from 1850 to 1870, although most of these combinations have had little permanent effect on the shape of modern New Zealand English. (This is obviously true of Mrs German's combination of features, for instance – modern New Zealand English does have a distinction between the vowels of LOT and THOUGHT.) One very good example from among the ONZE speakers is provided by Mr Malcolm Ritchie, who was born in 1866 in Cromwell of parents who came from Perthshire, Scotland, and who has a phonological system which sounds very bizarre to anyone familiar with British Isles varieties of English, combining features of Irish and/or Scottish origin with features that are obviously of English English origin. For example, in his speech /θ/ and /ð/ are often realised as dental stops, as in Irish English, and /t/ is often dental before /r/ – for example, in *tree* and *water*. Syllable-final /l/ may also be clear, as in Irish English (and also, as we saw in Chapter 2, in earlier forms of English English). On the other hand, he also has H Dropping, which never occurs in Irish English, and, even more bizarrely, his H Dropping is combined with the presence of the distinction between /ʍ/ and /w/, as in *which* and *witch*. This combination is currently totally unknown in the British Isles, where only those accents such as Scots and Northumbrian which have retained /h/ also retain /ʍ/, but where the reverse is not necessarily the case, as we noted in Chapter 2. Mr Ritchie also pronounces *wasn't* as *wadn* – something which, in Britain, is associated only with the southwest of England (see Chapter 1). We note, in this connection, that there was an area of Cromwell which was known at the time as 'Cornishtown' because of the Cornish miners who lived there (Cornwall being the southwesternmost county of England).

Similarly, Mrs H. Ritchie, born in 1863 in Arrowtown, Otago, combines Scottish features with some very non-Scottish features. Her accent, for example, is rhotic, and /r/ is realised in most environments as a partially unvoiced tap [ɾ̥], which I interpret as Highland Scottish in origin – she pronounces *here* as [hiəɾ̥], *square* as [skweəɾ̥]. She has /hw/ in *which*, etc., pronounces *with* with /θ/ and does not distinguish the vowels of FOOT and GOOSE. On the other hand, she has very Diphthong Shifted realisations of /au/ and /ai/. These are typical of the south of England generally and, in conjunction with the Scottish features, strike the British Isles listener as highly anomalous: the contrast between Cockney-style Glide Weakened /au/ = [æə] (see Chapter 6) and the expected Scottish [ɜʉ] as in *out* is extremely apparent. It is an indication of the possibilities open to children in dialect-mixture situations, such as that which obtained in Arrowtown (see below) in the 1860s, that it is perhaps not too fanciful to suppose that Mrs Ritchie may be the only English speaker ever in the history of the language to have said things like *out here* [æət hiəɾ̥]!

Intra-individual variability

In Trudgill (1986a: 108), I hypothesised that speakers who have grown up in a complex dialect-mixture situation are likely to demonstrate idiolects with considerable *intra*-individual variability, to a much greater extent than speakers from more stable, homogeneous speech communities. Given that the Mobile Unit recordings provide empirical confirmation of the hypothesis concerning original combinations of features, it is not too surprising to discover confirmation also for this hypothesis concerning intra-individual variability. Care does have to be taken at this point, it is true, since some such variability may be the result of accommodation to the speech of younger New Zealanders during the informants' long lifetimes. Nevertheless, the amount of variability in the speech of many of these individuals is very striking indeed, and strongly suggestive that idiolects formed in dialect-mixture situations may be much more variable than idiolects formed in stable speech communities.

For example, Mr Riddle, who was born in Palmerston, Otago, in 1860, shows an astonishing degree of variability:

1. His accent is rhotic but only variably so.
2. He demonstrates some very un-Scottish H Dropping, but this is highly inconsistent.

Neither of these two facts are, perhaps, particularly surprising – most British H Droppers are variably so, and there are many parts of the world, notably southwestern England, where many rhotic-accented speakers have only variable rhoticity. The remaining features, however, are most unusual:

3. /æ/ as in TRAP can be either – and this is particularly astonishing – [ɛ] or [a] (but not [æ]!);
4. /iː/ as in FLEECE varies between the short monophthong [i], typical of Scots, and a long diphthong [əi], typical of southern England – and individual lexical items can occur with both pronunciations;
5. /ei/ and /ou/ as in FACE and GOAT alternate between very Scottish monophthongal pronunciations, with [e] and [o], and very un-Scottish pronunciations, with the wide diphthongs [æɪ] and [ʌʊ];
6. similarly, /ai/, as in PRICE, alternates between a typical Scottish diphthong [ɜɪ] and an open central monophthong [ʌː], halfway between cardinal 4 and 5 in quality, whose provenance is not entirely clear but could be Lancashire.

The most likely explanation would appear to be that Mr Riddle grew up in a community providing both English English and Scottish English models and that, for some phonological features, he acquired both variants. Mr Riddle is by no means the only speaker to display this kind of behaviour.

Inter-individual variability

The extent to which individual choices can be made at Stage II, in the period prior to focussing, is further demonstrated by the extent to which people who have grown up in the same place at the same time may differ very markedly from one another. A dramatic illustration of this is provided by our recordings from Arrowtown.

Mrs H. Ritchie, who was mentioned above and who was born in

1863, and Mr R. Ritchie, who was born in 1864, went to school together in Arrowtown and became brother- and sister-in-law. They lived close to each other and remained in close contact all their lives. Nevertheless, they differ from one another in their phonologies in a way which one would not expect at all in a more stable situation. Mr Ritchie, for example, distinguishes between [eˑ] reflexes of ME ā as in *gate* and [ɛɪ] reflexes of ME *ai* as in *chain*. Mrs Ritchie, on the other hand, does not have this feature at all, but she has consistently close realisations of /æ/ as [ɛ] as in TRAP, and /ɛ/ as [e] as in DRESS, while Mr Ritchie typically has more open realisations. Both speakers are rhotic but Mrs Ritchie most often has /r/ as [ɻ], as we just saw, whereas Mr Ritchie favours a more English English-type [ɹ].

The full extent of the variability present in this community can be revealed more dramatically by an examination of a number of key variables. Recordings of nine speakers, including Mrs Ritchie and Mr Ritchie, all born in Arrowtown in the twenty-three-year period between 1863 and 1886, show astonishing variability for certain consonants, particularly bearing in mind that all the speakers knew each other well, and in many cases were related and/or had grown up and gone to school together. Some speakers, for instance, have H Dropping but others do not. Some speakers are rhotic but others are not, and four quite distinct realisations of /r/ occur: [ɻ], [ɹ], [ɻ] and [ɾ]. Some speakers distinguish between *which* and *witch*, while others fail to make the distinction. Some speakers have clear /l/ in all positions and others have both clear /l/ and dark /l/ distributed allophonically. Some speakers voice and flap intervocalic /t/ but others do not.

There is also relatively little implicational predictability. The possibility of each speaker developing individual combinations means that, for example, amongst our nine speakers, we have some who combine the THOUGHT vowel in *off* with voiceless *th* in *with*; some who combine it with voiced *th* in *with*; and some who combine the LOT vowel in *off* with voiced *th*.

The most striking amount of variability, though, occurs with the vowels. We can detect vowel qualities associated with Irish English, Scottish English, and regional English English occurring seemingly at random, with some individual speakers using more than one variant. Using the keywords introduced by Wells (1982), we can

note the following phonetically quite distinct variants in Arrowtown:

KIT:	[ɨ]	[ɪ]	[i]		
DRESS:	[ɛ]	[e]			
KIT:	[ɨ]	[ɪ]	[i]		
DRESS:	[ɛ]	[e]			
TRAP:	[æ]	[ɛ]			
STRUT:	[ə]	[ɐ]	[æ̞]		
LOT:	[ɒ]	[ɑ]			
FLEECE:	[iː]	[əi]			
FACE:	[eˑ]	[eˑⁱ]	[eɪ]	[ɛɪ]	[æɪ]
PRICE:	[aɪ]	[ɑɪ]	[ɑˑⁱ]	[ɑ̞ɛ]	[ɑˑɛ]
GOOSE:	[uː]	[ʉː]	[ʉː]	[əʉ]	
GOAT:	[oˑ]	[oˑᵘ]	[ou]	[ɔʊ]	[əʉ] [ɐˑʊ]
MOUTH:	[ɜʉ]	[ɛʉ]	[ɛʊ]	[ɛˑᵘ]	[æʊ] [æˑə]
NEAR:	[iˑɾ]	[iəɹ]	[iʲə]	[iə]	[ɪəɹ] [ɪə]
SQUARE:	[eˑɾ]	[eʲə]	[eə]	[ɛəɹ]	[ɛə] [eəɹ]
NURSE:	[ɜːɹ]	[ɜː]	[θː]		
START:	[aː]	[aː]			

Even in highly stratified and complex urban societies, we would be
very surprised indeed to find this degree of variability between nine
speakers all from the same area. It is all the more remarkable, then,
that we find this degree of variation in a single small town amongst
people all of approximately the same age.

I have cited accommodation as being a key mechanism in the
Stage I rudimentary levelling process. Can we also see a role for
accommodation here at Stage II? It seems not. The considerable
inter-individual variability characterising the speakers of this
generation means that they demonstrably did not indulge in long-
term accommodation to one another. The variability that we witness
here is certainly, rather, the result of children selecting at will from
a kind of supermarket, as it were, of vocalic and consonantal variants
with which they were surrounded. We have to say, then, that what
occurred was a form of variable acquisition, not accommodation.

APPARENT LEVELLING

I also assume, however, that inter-individual variability of this type, although striking and considerable, is somewhat reduced compared to what was present during the first stage (for which we have no recorded evidence). That is, in spite of all the variability we witness in the ONZE Corpus, it is probable that a process which resembles levelling has already occurred, in addition to the rudimentary levelling which was discussed in the previous chapter. We have no direct evidence of this, but there are some features which we can be sure must have been brought to New Zealand by significant numbers of immigrating speakers, but which are nevertheless not present in the ONZE Corpus. I am not referring here to minority Traditional-dialect features such as the /v/–/w/ merger, mentioned above as having been removed through rudimentary levelling. Rather, I am supposing that there were other more mainstream regional English features which were sufficiently common that they must have actually survived the initial contact stage. The puzzle is, therefore, why are such features nevertheless absent, or almost so, from the ONZE recordings?

One such feature is the use of the FOOT vowel in the lexical sets of both FOOT and STRUT, indicating a system of five rather than six short, checked vowels. As we saw in Chapter 2, this feature was at the relevant time, and still is, normal in middle-class as well as working-class accents in nearly all of England north of a line from the Bristol Channel to the Wash – an area comprising approximately half the geographical surface of England and containing approximately half its population. We can therefore assume that, as a major and widespread accent feature found in England in the speech of many millions of people, this system would have made it, unlike the Traditional-dialect features discussed earlier, to New Zealand without being levelled out on the boat or soon after arrival. Only one of my eighty-four informants, however, has this feature.

Another geographically widespread feature which is more or less totally absent from our data is the centralised KIT vowel of Lowland Scottish English. As we saw in Chapter 2, many forms of Scottish English have KIT as a low or mid central vowel. In Trudgill (1986a), I argued that the New Zealand English central KIT vowel, which also occurs as an allophonic variant in South African English, was the result of Scottish English input into the dialect mixtures that eventually led to the development of this feature in these Southern Hemisphere varieties. I now have to concede that it is very clear indeed from the ONZE recordings that my thesis concerning the Scottish origins of /ɪ/ as a central vowel is incorrect. In the ONZE corpus, even those Mobile Unit speakers who are most obviously and consistently Scottish in their phonetics and phonology do not have this feature. (I therefore also withdraw my suggestion about South African English.) However, it is legitimate to suppose that this feature must have *arrived* in New Zealand. As we have seen, 22% of the early migrants to New Zealand were Scots.

The Threshold Rider

The absence of these two features – a 5-short-vowel system and centralized KIT – from the ONZE data would appear to contradict what I have said in this chapter about the absence of accommodation at Stage II. I argue, however, that their absence is not in fact due to accommodation as such but to a phenomenon I will refer to as *apparent levelling*.

I suggest that what happened was the following. The north of England vowel system was certainly present in the Stage I dialect mixture but *not in sufficient quantities*. It is true that many millions of people had, and still have, this feature in England, but the north of England as a place of origin was under-represented amongst the immigrants to New Zealand. For the centralised KIT vowel, we can similarly suppose that, while present in the Stage I dialect mixture, it too was not prevalent enough for it to survive into Stage II. Many of the Scottish immigrants were Highlanders who did not have this feature and/or speakers who had educated accents: Wells (1982: 404) writes that the quality of the KIT vowel is 'in an educated Scottish accent much the same as in RP'.

I account for the absence of these features by proposing that there was some form of cut-off point at Stage II for variants which were only rather weakly represented in the Stage I input. Centralised KIT and the northern five-short-vowel system occurred with a frequency which was below some threshold necessary for perception and acquisition on the part of children at Stage II. It is difficult to calculate what this threshold might be, but it could perhaps have been something like 10%. So, although these forms did in fact survive in the speech of immigrant adults, they occurred at too low a level of frequency to be *noticed* by children at Stage II – they were not present in sufficient numbers to attract the children's attention. (On *noticing* as a technical term, see Schmidt, 1990.) As Nettle (1999: 23) says in a discussion of direction in linguistic change, 'certain variants are so rare as to be impossible to acquire'. This, then, is what gave rise – without accommodation – to the phenomenon of apparent levelling at Stage II. I call it 'apparent levelling' because the effect – a reduction in the number of variants – is indeed identical with the effect of levelling. However, the mechanism that was involved in achieving this reduction was different. It was not the case that variants acquired by speakers were removed from the mixture as a result of speakers accommodating to one another; rather, these variants were simply not acquired at all in the first place.

I also distinguish between features subject to apparent levelling and those subject to rudimentary levelling because I surmise that the former would have been maintained in the speech of many adults at Stage I, throughout their lifetimes, while very localised Traditional-dialect features would mostly have been removed from their speech. However, recall from Chapter 3 that we supposed that adults would not have been totally successful in removing Traditional-dialect features from their speech, and so tokens of such variants would have occurred from time to time. The threshold effect would also, therefore, have been operative in helping to ensure that variants of this type at Stage I would not have survived into Stage II either.

Notice that the concept of the 'threshold' has a respectable pedigree in historical linguistics. Lightfoot (1999: 155–6), in his Universal Grammar approach to grammatical change, suggests a dialect-contact context for the change away from verb-second structures in northern medieval English:

> Children in Lincolnshire and Yorkshire, as they mingled with southerners, would have heard sentences whose initial elements were non-subjects followed by a finite verb less frequently than the required threshold ... the evidence suggests that 17% of initial non-subjects does not suffice to trigger a verb-second grammar, but 30% is enough.

I hypothesise that, at levels lower than the threshold, idiosyncrasies might be passed on from one generation to another in an unpredictable, non-deterministic way, but that systematic features will not be. Mrs German, for example, acquired the East Anglian short 'o' only in her pronunciation of a single lexical item – *home*, pronounced /hʊm/ – but she did not acquire this feature systematically across the lexicon. We can assume that this was because its level of occurrence in her community generally – being present perhaps in the speech of her parents and of no one else – was not sufficiently high for her to do so.

CHAPTER 5

Stage III – determinism in new-dialect formation

The third stage in the development of colonial Englishes is represented by the arrival at the final, stable, relatively uniform outcome of the new-dialect formation process. As far as New Zealand English is concerned, this outcome was achieved, approximately, in the speech of those born around 1890. For the phonology, this final outcome is equivalent to contemporary New Zealand English minus the twentieth-century innovations listed in Chapter 2.

It is at the third stage, then, that the new dialect appears as a stable, crystallised variety. This crystallisation is the result, as discussed earlier, of a focussing process (Le Page and Tabouret-Keller, 1985). However, the big question is why the koinéisation which preceded this focussing took the precise form that it did. In particular, why did the levelling that was part of the koinéisation process take the form that it took?

THE SURVIVAL OF MAJORITY FORMS

I claimed above that situations involving transplantation and contact between mutually intelligible dialects lead to the development of new dialects out of a dialect-mixture situation through a process whereby the large numbers of variants from the different dialects involved in the mixture are reduced in number, until usually only one variant remains for each variable. This levelling takes place as a result of group accommodation between speakers in face-to-face interaction. But exactly how does this reduction in the number of variants take place? Why were certain forms retained and others lost? This is not a question that students of new-dialect formation have always thought to ask. Mougeon and Beniak (1994: 26) discuss 'features of the French varieties spoken in New France which were present at the beginning of the history of the colony ... but *which have not survived*' (their italics, my translation). They then go on to suggest that too many French Canadian studies have concentrated on features of modern Quebec French, and their origins in France, without considering why other competing features died out. They point out, for example, that in the French dialect input to Quebec French, words from the lexical set of *poulet* 'chicken' (Standard French /pule/) would have had five different variants as far as the final vowel was concerned: forms ending in /-e, -ɛ, -o, -ɔ/ and /-a/. The form that survived in Québécois (unlike in Standard French) was the variant in /-a/. What, they ask, happened to all the others?

My position, as noted above, is that reduction does not take place in a haphazard manner. The obvious way to investigate this claim about the non-random nature of levelling and to examine the major process of variant-reduction – that is, the reduction which occurred at Stage III for New Zealand English and which removed all variants in each case except one – is to compare the speech of the ONZE Project informants to that of modern New Zealanders. When we compare the variable and varied speech of the ONZE Project speakers to the focussed speech of modern New Zealanders, it becomes clear that the crucial explanatory factor for the way levelling takes place is *the survival of majority variants*, as has already been suggested in Chapter 3. The final shape of New Zealand English is the result of a levelling process which, for the most part, consisted of the loss of demographically minority forms.

Again, the crucial actors at this stage were children. Adults of the previous generation, at Stage II, did not, as we have seen, speak New Zealand English as such at any stage of their lives, although they were born and lived all their lives in New Zealand. We can assume that this was because they were presented as young children with a bewildering array of linguistic variants to choose from. At Stage III, on the other hand, in a more stable social situation and with a more restricted set of variants to choose from, children selected from among the smaller array of variants they were confronted with on a rational, although still subconscious, basis. They simply selected, in most cases, the variants which were most common.

This deterministic, non-random view of what happened implies that, although New Zealand English is a variety which is, from a phonological point of view, basically a southeast-of-England sort typologically, this is *not* because most of the immigrants from Britain to New Zealand came from rural Essex (an absurd claim) or from the English southeast generally (less absurd), but because, as it happens, individual forms found in the southeast of England were also, coincidentally, very often majority forms in the original dialect mixture.

There is a parallel to this, as Mougeon and Beniak (1994: 33) point out, with Canadian French. The French of Quebec is rather similar to the French of the Île de France but, at points where the forms of varieties from this area were in a minority, they did not survive – for example, as we just saw, Québécois has *poulet* /pula/ rather than Île de France /pule/. Where an Île de France variant did not survive, this was 'because it came up against a widespread vernacular rural pronunciation' (my translation).

Note that my espousal of this thesis means that I do not accept Lass's (1990) notion of *swamping* as an explanation for the predominance of southeastern forms in South African English: by swamping, Lass means the consistent selection by colonial speakers of forms from the English southeast, when faced with a number of alternatives.

It is crucial for my thesis that there are a number of cases in all three major Southern Hemisphere varieties where southeast-of-England forms were *not* in a majority, and where they therefore did *not* survive. A considerable number of non-southeastern forms have survived in modern New Zealand English (in addition to obvious lexical features of the type discussed by Bauer (2000) such as Scottish *wee* versus English English *small*), and we now move on to discuss the most crucial of these features.

Non-southeastern features

H Retention

H Dropping does not survive in New Zealand English in spite of
the fact that it was the norm in vernacular nineteenth-century
varieties in London, and everywhere else in the southeast of England.
The ONZE data explain why this should have happened: although
H Dropping is not uncommon on the recordings, only a minority of
the speakers (about 25%) use this feature. And our discussions in
Chapter 2 can, in turn, explain why *this* was so: the Irish, Scottish,
Northumbrian, West Country, East Anglian and other English
dialects with H Retention were in the majority in the original dialect
mixture (see Map 9), and therefore this feature has won out in
modern New Zealand English at the expense of the minority southeastern form. (This is, then, also an example of evidence for the
concealed influence of Irish and Scottish English mentioned earlier.)
Immigration figures help to confirm this thesis. Even if all the
immigrants from Wales and England combined were H Droppers,
they would have constituted only around half of the arrivals, and
would therefore have been matched numerically by arrivals from
Scotland and Ireland, areas where H Dropping was and is still
unknown. And, of course, they would not all have been H Droppers:
many of the English immigrants would have been from those areas
shown on Map 9 as still preserving /h/. There is thus a high proba-
bility that, during the crucial Stage I formation period, H Droppers
in New Zealand were in a minority, unlike in the southeast of England. Similar points could be made for Australia and South Africa
which also, by and large, lack H Dropping.

It is also relevant that, for nearly all speakers who have this
feature, H Dropping is variable: there are very few speakers who
drop a hundred per cent of /h/s. This is true of modern England and
Wales, and it is true of the 25% of speakers on the ONZE recordings. We can therefore suppose that H Dropping percentages would
also have been influential: we are really talking about tokens here as
well as about speakers – speakers who had low H Dropping
percentages would have been more easily outnumbered, as it were,
by non-H Droppers than speakers with high percentages.

Absence of Glide Cluster Reduction

Another southeast-of-England feature which did not survive into modern New Zealand English was the merger of /w/ and /ʍ/ as in *which, where, white*. (It is true that this merger is now appearing in modern New Zealand English, but this seems to be a recent phenomenon – see Turner, 1966.) Here again, we can advance the same explanation – and this in spite of mergers having an advantage over distinctions. Although the English of southeastern England and, probably, Australia had merged *whales* and *Wales*, it was the Scottish, Irish and northern England form which was the one to survive the levelling process. This survival was, once again, for purely demographic reasons – there were more speakers with than without the distinction between /w/ and /ʍ/. This point is confirmed by the analysis of nineteenth-century British Isles English portrayed in Map 10 (and bearing in mind that Ireland is not actually shown on that map).

Absence of START Backing

A similar case is provided by START Backing (Wells, 1982: 234). As we saw earlier, the English of London and the southeast of England has a back vowel [ɑ:] in this lexical set. Australian and New Zealand English, on the other hand, have a very front quality, [a:]. The ONZE Project data explain why this is. Speakers on the ONZE tapes demonstrate a whole range of realisations of the vowel in START, from very front through central to back, but front realisations are the more common on the recordings. This is why they have been the ones to survive. And we can further explain why front qualities are the more common in the ONZE Project data by looking at Map 7 in Chapter 2: obviously, front variants were much more common in nineteenth-century Britain than back variants. The southeastern variant was in the minority and is, therefore, not present in modern Australasian English.

The Weak Vowel Merger

The contention that New Zealand English is not simply transported southeast-of-England English is further confirmed by the surprising, on the face of it, but (I claim) predictable fact that yet another

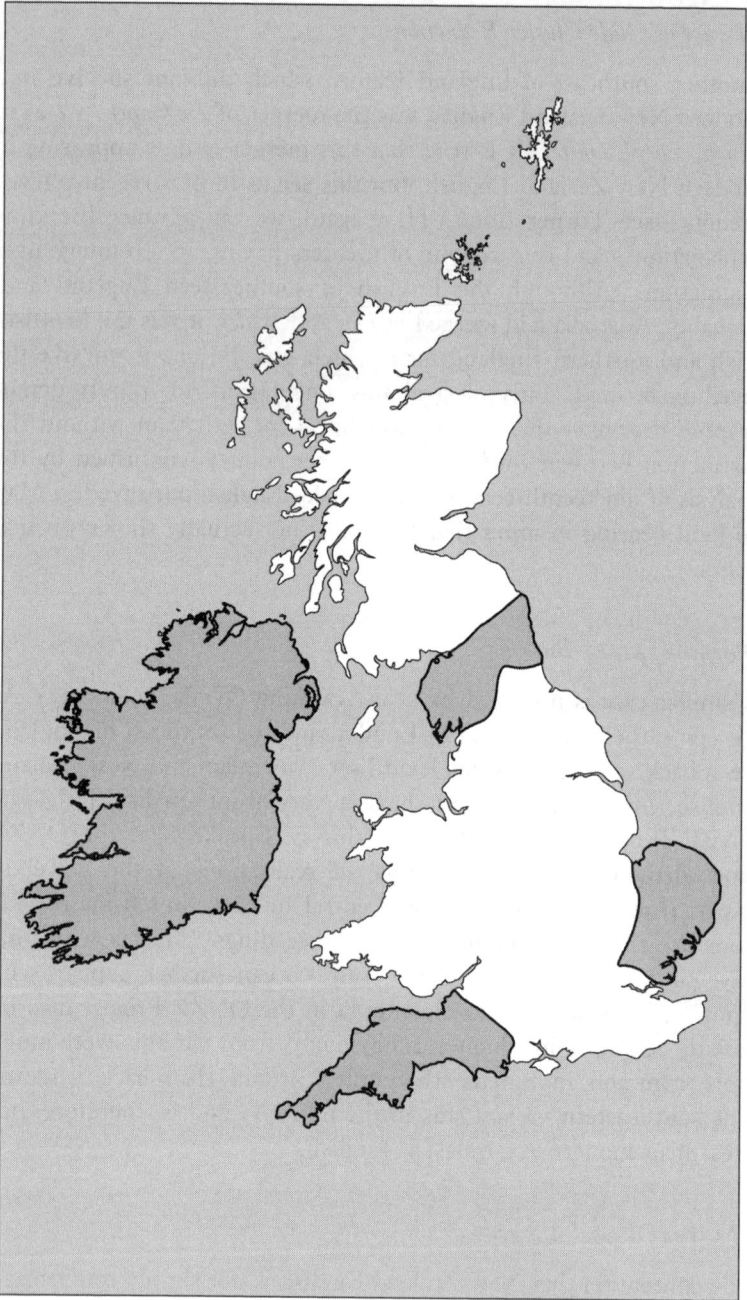

Map 11: Shaded areas: regions of the British Isles with Weak Vowel Merger (after Trudgill, 1999)

southeast-of-England form did not survive in New Zealand English even though it *was* in the majority in the dialect mixture. One obvious and very important difference between New Zealand, Australian, South African, Falkland Islands and Tristan da Cunha English, on the one hand, and that of the southeast of England, on the other, is that the Southern Hemisphere Englishes have /ə/ in unstressed syllables in all or nearly all cases where southeast England has /ɪ/. The Southern Hemisphere Englishes have no contrast between *Lenin* and *Lennon*; the English of London does. Southeastern English English has /ɪ/ in the unstressed syllables of *Lenin, David, market, wanted, changes, walkin', service, hate it, like 'im* etc. while Southern Hemisphere English has /ə/. This Southern Hemisphere English phenomenon is referred to by Wells (1982: 167) as the Weak Vowel Merger. In accents which have this merger, pairs such as *abbot* and *rabbit* rhyme. (This point is further complicated in modern New Zealand English by the centralisation of the KIT vowel, which has led to a merger with schwa, but this is a twentieth-century development and can be ignored here.)

In the initial dialect mixture that eventually produced the Southern Hemisphere Englishes, speakers from Ireland (which clearly played a crucial role here), East Anglia, the West Country and the far north of England would have had schwa in unstressed syllables of words such as *rabbit*, while speakers using forms from Scotland, the London region and the central areas of England would have had /ɪ/. This is indicated in Map 11, which is based on data in Trudgill (1999) which is, in turn, based on the SED materials from the 1950s and 1960s.

Presumably as a consequence of this distribution, in the ONZE Corpus schwa is very common in the unstressed syllables of words like *hundred, hunted, naked, rabbit, horses*. However, it is not the majority form: only 32% of the ONZE Project informants use schwa in such items. Nevertheless, as I have stressed (in Chapter 3 and in Trudgill, 1986), unmarked forms may survive at the expense of marked forms, even if they are in a minority, and clearly schwa is the unmarked vowel par excellence. The large minority of 32% of ONZE Project informants at Stage II, I suggest, was high enough for it to replace other forms at the Stage III on the grounds of its unmarkedness.

The reduction of variants over time is thus not haphazard from the point of view of purely linguistic forces, either: degrees of linguistic markedness may be involved, such that unmarked forms may have the edge in the competition for survival over marked forms. I referred to this above as *unmarking*. It seems, too, that this principle also has a more general application: following Trudgill (1986a), Mufwene (2001: 58) has proposed a markedness model as an explanatory factor in creole genesis also.

I acknowledge, of course, that markedness has to be used as an explanatory factor with care. Mostly, it is majority forms that survive, regardless of whether they are relatively marked or not. H Retention, for example, survives even though pronunciations with /h/ are clearly more marked than pronunciations without. My suggestion is simply that unmarkedness may sway the balance in favour of minority variants, provided, obviously, that they are a large minority.

Word phonology

I am much less inclined to argue deterministically when it comes to the pronunciation of individual words. Nevertheless, the following example is interesting. In the English of modern England, *with* is pronounced with /ð/. In Scotland and Ireland, on the other hand, it is pronounced with final /θ/. (American English accents vary on this point.) Immigration figures would suggest that English /ð/ pronouncers would have outnumbered Scottish and Irish /θ/ pronouncers in early New Zealand. However, the voiceless consonant is the one which is most common on our ONZE recordings and which has survived into most forms of modern New Zealand English. It is also found in Falkland Islands English. (Tristanian does not have either /θ/ or /ð/ – having /s/, /f/ or /d/ instead – and so is irrelevant at this point.) This suggests, rather strongly, that some geographically peripheral varieties of English English still had the voiceless consonant in *with* in the mid-nineteenth century and subsequently lost it, and that the southeast of England lost out here to other areas of England, plus Scotland and Ireland, purely on a demographic basis.

Southeastern features

The short front vowels

In many other cases, of course, the variant from the English southeast did survive. However, my point is that this only happened if these variants *also* had support, as it were, from other areas of the British Isles. For example, the vowels of KIT, DRESS, TRAP have a very wide range of realisations on the ONZE Project recordings (though, as we have seen, centralised KIT is absent). However, the closer variants [i, e, ɛ] which are typical of nineteenth-century southeastern England (see Chapter 2) are much more common on the recordings than the more open variants associated with the north of England, Scotland and Ireland. Sixty per cent of the ONZE Project speakers have DRESS and TRAP vowels which are closer than [ɛ] and [æ] respectively – and it is again therefore no surprise that these won out. However, approximately 43% of immigrants came to New Zealand from Scotland and Ireland, where the DRESS and TRAP vowels typically have a rather open quality, and this would also have been true of English people from parts of the West Country and the North. It is therefore probable that the closer vowels would not have ended up being in the majority unless support had been available from outside southeastern England also. I suggest that, in this case, support for the southeastern forms came from three sources. One would have been East Anglia; the second would have been the Australian input into the dialect mixture (as we saw in Chapter 2, Australian English also has close variants); and the third would have been from the interdialectal substitution by adults at Stage I of the Scottish DRESS vowel in TRAP words, as discussed in Chapter 3.

Diphthong Shift

As far as Diphthong Shift is concerned, the geographical pattern outlined in Chapter 2 shows that, although the centre of diffusion was London, this feature was not, by the mid-nineteenth century, just a southeastern feature. Given that it extended beyond the English southeast, and given what we know about the demographics of the immigration to New Zealand, it is not surprising that Diphthong Shifted forms are very common in the ONZE data. In all, 75% of the Mobile Unit speakers have phonologies which are characterised by Diphthong Shifting of at least some diphthongs. Here again the majority forms won, as they did also in Australia and South Africa, but the southeast did require support from the English Midlands and neighbouring areas of the southwest and East Anglia for that to be the case.

The rounded LOT vowel

In at least two cases in the growth of New Zealand English, survival of one variant rather than another on demographic grounds must have been somewhat touch-and-go.

First we saw, in Chapter 2, that an unrounded vowel in the set of LOT was probably much more common in English English in the nineteenth century than it is today. Unrounded /ɒ/ in LOT = [ɑ] is very common in the ONZE recordings: 47% of the informants use a non-southeastern unrounded vowel either consistently or variably. The fact that it has disappeared from modern New Zealand English has to be ascribed to the fact that users of the rounded variant were in a rather small majority, i.e. 53%.

/a:/ in DANCE

Even more interesting is what has happened in the case of the vowel in the lexical set of DANCE. It is well known that accents of English treat lexical items such as *dance, laugh, path, plant* in two different ways. Accents in the north of England and North America have /æ/ in such words, while RP and accents in the south of England have /a:/. This is the result of Pre-Fricative Lengthening (see Chapter 2). I argued in Chapter 2 that we are in fact dealing here with two separate sound changes, one in simple pre-fricative environments, and another in pre-nasal environments. Evidence in support of this thesis from the ONZE recordings is overwhelming: excluding speakers, as we obviously must, who do not have a distinction between /æ/ and /a:/ – presumably as a result of West Country and/or Scottish input – very many ONZE speakers consistently have southeastern /a:/ in the lexical set of *after, grass, path*, but northern and Midland /æ/ in the set of *dance, plant, sample*. Of the eligible speakers (that is, those who do have two contrastive vowels at this point), 48% have this pattern. In the end, in modern New Zealand

English, it was the southeastern and East Anglian pattern used by the other 52% of the ONZE Project informants which won out. But it must have been a close-run thing, and input from the English southeast on its own would probably not have been sufficient for this to have occurred.

Conclusion

Further support for the determinism thesis is found at the level of grammar. Of the nonstandard grammatical forms cited in Chapter 1, only those which are common *throughout* the British Isles (and indeed, as it happens, throughout the English-speaking world in general) are the ones to survive in modern New Zealand English – such as preterite *come*, preterite main verb *done*, and multiple negation. There is no trace in modern New Zealand English of, for example, the Irish English *after* construction or of southwest-of-England present-tense *be*.

It seems, then, that most of what occurred in between the second and third generation of New Zealand English speakers was simply the levelling out of minority variants such as H Dropping. Nettle (1999: 22) observes:

> Children learn language partly in order to keep in kilter with the speech norms of their social group. It is, therefore, reasonable to assume that, during language acquisition, they will home in as accurately as possible on the speech going on around them. The optimum learning strategy for them would, therefore, be some kind of error-minimizing procedure – that is, an algorithm for minimizing the discrepancy between the child's own speech and that which it hears going on around it. Error-minimizing strategies of this kind are likely to lead to children producing a statistical composite of the speech they experience.

Nettle is, of course, thinking here of a 'normal' non-mixed speech community. I suggest that my findings, and my argument for determinism in new-dialect formation, are simply the result of exactly the same sort of process occurring in a community with massive dialect mixture and no single peer-group norm. The new colonial dialects are a *statistical composite* of the dialect mixture.

REALLOCATION

The fact that the ONZE *dance* /æ/ versus /aː/ percentages were so close – see above – perhaps also sheds some light on the current situation in Australian English. As we have seen, one of the key new-dialect formation processes is *reallocation* (Trudgill, 1986a: 110; Britain and Trudgill, 1999). That is, in some instances, the number of variants present in a mixture may be reduced to two (or more) rather than to one. In such cases, the remaining variants are allocated different functions – typically sociolinguistic or, in the case of phonetics, allophonic. Unlike New Zealand English, Australian English has retained – and reallocated – both pronunciations of the set of *dance*, with – to simplify somewhat – the /aː/ vowel being associated with rather more prestigious varieties, and /æ/ with lower-status varieties: Wells writes (1982: 599) that many Australians 'consider /aː/ high-class, even indicative of affectation, pedantry, or snobbishness'. If the range of inputs to Australian English was similar to that found in the ONZE Corpus, it is not surprising that both variants survived: a sensible guess would be that reallocation is most likely to occur where two variants are present in the original mixture in roughly equal proportions. An interesting question, however, is why reallocation occurred in Australia but not in New Zealand: Wall (1938: 29) describes both vowels as 'equally good' for New Zealand English, suggesting that, in fact, alternation persisted for many decades there. Given that the consistent use of /aː/ in both sets of lexical items in modern South African English can probably be accounted for by the fact that it had a later formation date than that of Australian English, we can suppose that the difference between Australia and New Zealand can also be accounted for in the same way – later on in the nineteenth century, the pronunciation with /aː/ had become more common in Britain.

The notion of reallocation may also be relevant in New Zealand English with respect to the CLOTH vowel, as this was discussed in Chapter 2. As we saw earlier, Wells (1982: 203) dates Pre-Fricative Lengthening to the end of the seventeenth century, and the *Survey of English Dialects* shows the whole of the south of England as having /ɔː/ in this lexical set. The ONZE speakers pronounce the lexical set of *off, froth, cross* predominantly with /ɔː/ rather than /ɒ/. In fact, 70% of the informants, excluding the fourteen speakers who have the Scottish system (such as Mrs German) which does not distinguish between the vowels of LOT and THOUGHT, use this form at least sometimes. Interestingly, moreover, variability in this feature is still a characteristic of modern New Zealand English. We can therefore claim that this variability must have been a feature of New Zealand English from the outset, including variability between speakers *and* between lexical items. We can argue that both variants survived the levelling process in New Zealand because the number of relevant lexical items involved was small and because, if, as we suppose, the ONZE Project informants are representative of the total population, the overall proportion of the total informants (including the Scottish-system speakers) who actually had the short vowel in the relevant set was 57%, just a little more than half.

RANDOMNESS AND TRANSMISSION IN NEW-DIALECT FORMATION

I have argued, then, that new-dialect formation is deterministic in the sense that the outcome is predictable from the input. That is, the newly formed focussed dialect, which is the third-generation outcome of dialect contact and dialect mixture, is characterised, at least at the phonological level, by features which were in a majority in the input, except in cases where unmarked features are in a large minority and win out over majority features on the grounds of their unmarkedness.

Notice, however, that there is a fascinating problem concerning inter-generational transmission. We saw in Chapter 4 that, for ONZE Corpus speakers at the second stage of new-dialect formation, there was, in early communities, a kind of supermarket of vocalic and consonantal variants that they, as children, could pick and choose from and put together into new combinations. I suggested that is precisely why colonial and other new dialects consist, to a considerable extent, of new combinations of old features. It must also be true, of course, that patterns of interaction will have been important: for any individual child, people with whom he or she interacted most would have had more chance of influencing the final form of the child's speech than those who did not. But it is also clear that the inter-individual differences in the way in which these combinations were formed imply a degree of randomness concerning which speakers chose which variants. That is why different people in the same community arrive at different combinations, as we saw illustrated very clearly in the case of Arrowtown (see Chapter 4).

On the other hand, according to the theory of determinism in new-dialect formation, the survival of particular variants, such as /h/ as opposed to Ø, in modern New Zealand English is to be interpreted in terms of their majority status in the speech of the Stage II ONZE Project informants. And I, in turn, explain *this* in terms of the presumed majority status of these variants in the dialects brought to New Zealand by immigrants from different parts of the British Isles at the first stage. The differential proportions of variants in the ONZE Corpus (and thus their later survival or disappearance) is, in other words, *not* random. It is, as Nettle says, a 'statistical composite' of the speech the children were exposed to.

We therefore have to assume the following. The 'original' mixtures that were demonstrated for *individual* informants such as Mr Riddle at Stage II are indeed the result of random selection. But the proportions of variants present in the accents of groups of Stage II speakers in a particular location, *taken as a whole*, derive in a probabilistic manner from, and will therefore reflect – subject to the Threshold Rider – the proportions of the same variants present in the different varieties spoken by their parents' generation *taken as a whole*. The most common variants at Stage I were the ones which were most often selected at Stage II, even though Stage II speakers demonstrated considerable inter-individual variability stemming from freedom of choice; and these most common variants were therefore the ones to survive into Stage III – the new dialect we call New Zealand English.

For example, modern New Zealand English has both H Retention and /ʍ/ Retention. This is predictable from the fact that 75% of the Stage II ONZE Corpus informants were H Retainers and 60% were /ʍ/ Retainers, which is in turn because these were also approximately the proportions of such speakers, taken overall, at the earlier immigrant stage, the pre-ONZE Corpus Stage I. What was certainly *not* present at the first stage, of course, was the *combination* of H Dropping with retention of /ʍ/ demonstrated at the second stage by Mr Ritchie (unless perhaps Mr Ritchie's speech is representative of the small area of northwestern Yorkshire discussed earlier in connection with Maps 9 and 10). It is thus clear that accommodation is at its most vital at Stage III in the new-dialect formation process. Here, for each vowel and consonant variant, minority-variant users accommodate to majority-variant users as koinéisation progresses, and the majority form wins. Accommodation as a process is therefore clearly central to the new-dialect formation process. Note, however, that it is operative only at Stage I (by adults) and Stage III (by children), and not at the second stage of new-dialect formation, as already noted in Chapter 4. It should also be mentioned that in Trudgill (1986a) it was shown that accommodation was influenced by *salience*. In general, it is salient features which are accommodated to, as in the case of rudimentary levelling. It is therefore important to state here that salience does not seem to be relevant in determining what happens at Stages II and III in tabula rasa colonial situations. We do not see salient features being more 'successful' than others. And, indeed, the whole notion of salience would seem to be irrelevant here, since the way I perceived the concept was in terms of already established (adolescent and adult) linguistic systems. Speakers, I argued, are more aware of phonological features which are phonetically radically different from their own and/or which are involved in the maintenance of phonological contrasts in their own systems. This cannot be operative in a situation where young children do not yet have their 'own' phonologies. I also suggested that speakers are more aware of forms that are currently involved in linguistic change. This is also irrelevant in a situation where there is no agreed or established shared system for changes to occur in.

CONCLUSION

In his discussion of dialect levelling and homogenisation, Chambers (1995: 58) writes:

We would like to understand precisely how this homogenisation takes place. Which features of constituent accents are retained, and which ones are lost? In other words, what are the dynamics of homogenisation? Since no sociolinguists were present – or even existed – during the European imperialist era, we will probably have to wait for the planting of colonies in outer space for large-scale studies of the dynamics of homogenisation.

I suggest that, in the meantime, the ONZE Project data and analyses, and the theory of determinism in new-dialect formation, have gone some considerable way towards answering Chambers's questions. The determinism theory also explains the similarities between the different Southern Hemisphere varieties (although there is one other factor which we will cover in the following chapter): these varieties all developed from similar mixtures of British dialects, according to the same principle.

Insofar as they are different, on the other hand, this will reflect

differences in the specific compositions of the pools of features that competed with each other in these colonies. Even if the same features were taken to all these territories, their preference strengths relative to their competitors sometimes varied from one pool to another, which led to the selection and/or dominance of different variants from one new variety to another. (Mufwene, 2001: 158)

As Poirier (1994: 256) says, of North American French:

Quebec French, Acadian French and Louisiana French have a large number of characteristics in common ... but the combination of different dialect features took place in a different way in each of the three places because of the composition of the groups of settlers [my translation].

CHAPTER 6

Drift: parallel developments in the Southern Hemisphere Englishes

I have argued that the Southern Hemisphere Englishes, like most colonial Englishes, were initially the result of a series of dialect mixture and new-dialect formation processes. We need to acknowledge, however, that, as always, things must have been rather more complicated than that, and some of these issues are dealt with in the next chapter. Here we look at one very specific complication. I have suggested that the formative period for the development of the Southern Hemisphere Englishes was, in each case, a couple of generations, a time-span of fifty years. The time-span I suggested as constituting the formative period for the appearance of New Zealand English lasted from 1840 to 1890 approximately. The complication is that linguistic change must have continued to take place in the normal way during that fifty-year period, over and above the new-dialect formation processes at work during that time, and even bearing in mind the phenomenon of colonial lag (see Chapter 2).

For example, we saw in Chapter 1 that the ONZE Project archive data, in providing us with information about mid-nineteenth-century British Isles English, indicate that it was very common at that time to treat main verb *have* in the same way as auxiliary *have* – that is, it did not need *do*-support so that we found examples such as:

If they hadn't enough ...
She hadn't anything.
He hadn't a situation.

you haven't five pounds
I don't know how many roofs that old house hadn't.

This was the case even when dynamic meanings were involved:

They had a good time, hadn't they?

Two things about modern New Zealand English are therefore of considerable interest. First, modern New Zealand English, like most other varieties of English, today normally does require *do*-support for dynamic main verb *have*, suggesting changes in parallel in different parts of the English-speaking world.

Second, the change seems to be continuing. Attempts to show that there might be distinctive syntactic forms in modern New Zealand Standard English usually conclude by suggesting that, if there are any such differences at all, then they are simply a matter of differential rates of usage of particular constructions (Hundt, 1998).

Most studies of modern New Zealand English grammar suffer from the weakness that they are based on questionnaire responses to issues of usage and acceptability, rather than on observation. Happily, Hundt's study does not fall into this category. It is based on an analysis of written newspaper texts rather than on spoken usage, but it does have the value of shedding light on variability in contemporary New Zealand English. Most of this variability appears to be due to changes in progress, and it is of considerable interest that all of these changes appear to be paralleled by changes that are also occurring elsewhere in the English-speaking world (see Trudgill et al., 2002, where American English is also discussed). Of greatest interest to us here is the fact that New Zealand English appears, like English English, to be moving towards a system where, once again, dynamic and stative main verb *have* are treated the same grammatically but, this time, both are now requiring *do*-support (see the very useful summary in Quinn, 2000). We can portray this diagrammatically for both England and New Zealand thus:

19th c.   *Have you coffee with breakfast?*
          Have you any money?
20th c.   *Do you have coffee with breakfast?*
          Have you any money?

21st c. *Do you have coffee with breakfast?*
Do you have any money?

It is probable that the same development has occurred in Australian and South African English. We can regard these as changes in parallel in different parts of the anglophone world – changes in the language which have been set in motion and are continuing even after geographical separation.

THE THEORY OF DRIFT

I suggest that this phenomenon of parallel development in different parts of the English-speaking world is a clear example of what Sapir (1921) very insightfully labelled 'drift' (see also Lakoff, 1972). Sapir writes (p. 150) that 'language moves down time in a current of its own making. It has a drift.' More importantly for our purposes, he discusses inherent or inherited tendencies in languages and language families:

The momentum of ... drift is often such that languages long disconnected will pass through the same or strikingly similar phases ... The English type of plural represented by *foot: feet*, *mouse: mice* is strictly parallel to the German *Fuss: Füsse, Maus: Mäuse*. Documentary evidence shows conclusively that there could have been no plurals of this type in Primitive Germanic ... There was evidently some general tendency or group of tendencies in early Germanic, long before English and German had developed as such, that eventually drove both of these dialects along closely parallel paths. (p. 172)

I suggest that there are clear examples of similar phenomena in modern English.

In some versions, the drift theory has acquired rather mystical interpretations involving the 'spirit' or the 'genius' of the language (see also the reference to 'mysticism' in Lass, 1997: 301). I attempt here to demonstrate in a very concrete and, I like to think, down-to-earth way that 'drift happens', and to show what the relevance of Sapir's insight is to the history of colonial Englishes. I suggest that it is now actually possible, in the case of recently formed colonial Englishes, not only to deduce but actually to confirm that drift occurs; to produce contemporary illustrations of how drift operates; and to demonstrate, in more detail, how it happens.

Sapir's argument was essentially that language varieties may resemble one another because, having derived from some common source, they continue to evolve linguistically in similar directions by undergoing similar linguistic changes. If we accept Sapir's notion, we can argue that some similarities between different geographically separated varieties of English may, in some cases, be due not to their having derived from similar dialect mixtures, nor to characteristics inherited directly from some parent variety, nor to any diffusion or direct contact between them, but to drift. We have already noted three examples of this: we saw that English English and the Southern Hemisphere Englishes have experienced rhoticity loss in parallel; that Diphthong Shift is progressing in a number of varieties around the world; and that English RP has had pre-glottalisation since about 1900 (Andrésen, 1968) while North American English is only now beginning to acquire it (Andersen, 2002), even though there is no suggestion that American English has acquired it *from* British English. Similar phenomena appear in colonial varieties of other languages. Lipski (1994: 42) states, of South American Spanish, that 'some of the shared phonetic traits appear to have arisen independently in several areas'.

In the Southern Hemisphere Englishes, we can see examples of drift of two rather different types. In the first type, linguistic changes that are already in progress in the common source continue after separation. This type of drift includes Diphthong Shift (see Chapter 2) and loss of rhoticity, and is what Wells is referring to when he says that English in the Southern Hemisphere 'carries forward trends already present' in English English (1982: 593). In the second type, no linguistic change was underway in the common source, but varieties derived from it inherit shared *tendencies* or *propensities* which can subsequently lead to the development of similar but new changes, and hence similar or identical but new characteristics, even after separation, as with Sapir's umlaut plurals example. I make no claim for the theoretical status of these two different types: in any individual case, it may be difficult to determine whether changes really were actually in progress before a separation, or whether only the propensity to such a change was present. However, it is possible to see these two different types of drift phenomena exemplified in the Southern Hemisphere data.

NINETEENTH-CENTURY CHANGES ALREADY IN PROGRESS

Diphthong Shift in the Southern Hemisphere represents a continuation of changes already in progress in England and inherited from there. What is of interest is that all four Southern Hemisphere varieties of English – Australian, New Zealand, Falkland Islands and South African – not only inherited the results of these changes that had begun in England but also continued them after separation, often more rapidly than has been the case in Britain. There was a dynamism inherent in these ongoing changes which led to them continuing in parallel in the four different locations in the manner described by Sapir – although not always at the same speed, and not always coinciding in absolutely all details.

Fronted and lowered STRUT

Another such feature involves the vowel /ʌ/. As we have already noted, the STRUT vowel is a recent arrival in the phonological inventory of English, and many local varieties in England and southwestern Wales do not yet have it. As we also saw above, in the late 1500s the vowel /ʊ/ began to lose its lip-rounding in the southeast of England, giving [ɤ]. Subsequently, it lowered to [ʌ] – Gimson (1962: 103) postulates this 'for the eighteenth century' – and a vowel a little front of [ʌ] seems to have been the RP norm at the beginning of the twentieth century. During the course of the twentieth century, it then fronted to [ɐ] (although the practice continues of writing /ʌ/ to symbolise this vowel phonemically), which is the pronunciation in RP today (see Roach, 1983: 16). In the English of London and other parts of the southeast, however, the fronting has progressed further, giving 'an open front vowel very close to C [a]' (Gimson, 1962: 103). This diachronic pattern is reflected in a synchronic geographical pattern: the further one goes away from the English southeast, the further the vowel quality is located back along the trajectory the vowel has followed over the last 500 years (see Figure 4).

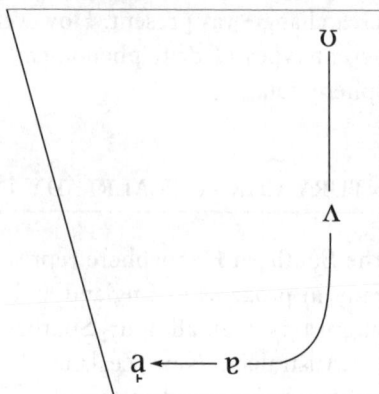

Figure 4: Change in the STRUT vowel

Map 12 shows areas of northern and midland England – plus Pembroke in southwest Wales – which have retained the original system of five short vowels. The border areas shown in Norfolk, Cambridgeshire, Northamptonshire, Oxfordshire and Gloucestershire constitute the region for which the SED shows southern pronunciations but which Ellis, seventy years earlier, gives as having the northern five-vowel system, at least variably. The area on the Scottish borders is the region shown by Ellis as having the Scottish system with /ʌ/, but by the SED as having the northern England five-vowel system. The larger area indicated in Northumberland and Durham is shown by Ellis as *variably* having /ʌ/, but is not so shown in the SED. We can therefore assume that, in the century between Ellis and SED, the southern system has moved slightly to the north in southern England, while the northern system has moved to the north to match up, more or less, with the Scottish–English border. (For more on this, see Trudgill, 1999; Ellis's map is best consulted in Ihalainen (1994: 236).) There is no evidence in the dialectological literature for STRUT Fronting, as such, but Map 12 also shows the area of the southeast of England for which Kurath and Lowman (1970: 17) show a 'fully unrounded and lowered' STRUT vowel, i.e. the most advanced form in their data.

It is therefore of considerable interest that modern New Zealand English typically has open and front realisations of this vowel. This is true of Australian English also. STRUT in Tristanian is also generally fronter than in RP. (STRUT Fronting is not a prominent feature of

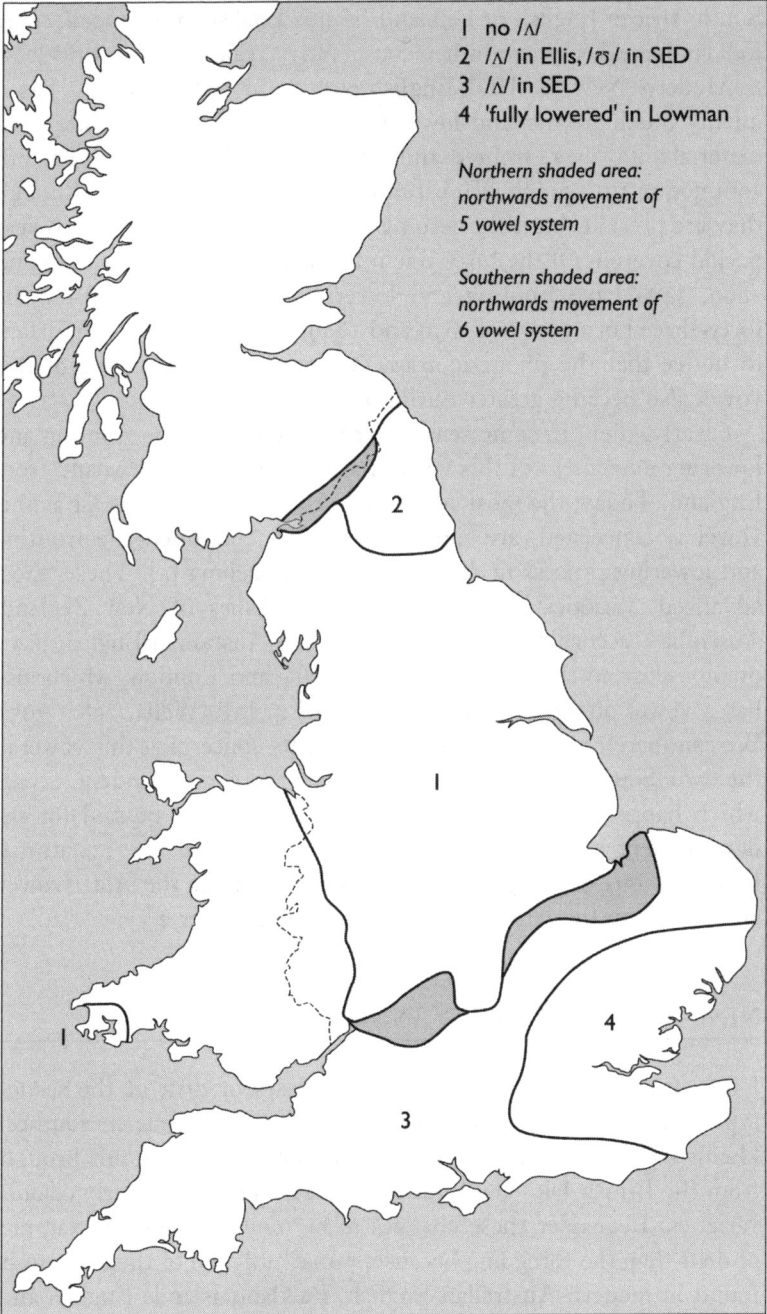

1 no /ʌ/
2 /ʌ/ in Ellis, /ʊ/ in SED
3 /ʌ/ in SED
4 'fully lowered' in Lowman

Northern shaded area:
northwards movement of
5 vowel system

Southern shaded area:
northwards movement of
6 vowel system

Map 12: The STRUT vowel

South African English or Falkland Islands English and, indeed, some Falkland speakers have rather conservative realisations around [ɜ].)

Modern New Zealand English STRUT, in fact, typically has a quality much fronter and lower even than [ɐ]. In the Mobile Unit materials, however, fronted and lowered vowels beyond [ɐ] are not common in the speech of most of our very oldest speakers, although they are present, but they become more common over the forty-year period covered. Of the forty-one informants born between 1850 and 1869, 34% have fronting and lowering, while the figure for the forty-three born between 1870 and 1889 is 40%. It is also important to notice that the phonetic *degree* of fronting and lowering of this vowel also became greater during the same time.

Clearly, then, in some sense a trend to continue the fronting and lowering movement of this vowel was brought to New Zealand from England. Today, the most advanced accents of English, as far as this vowel is concerned, are those which have continued the fronting and lowering process to reach a point approaching [a]. These 'most advanced' varieties are precisely the Englishes of New Zealand, Australia – according to Wells (1982: 599), Australian English has a quality close to the cardinal 4 vowel [a] – and London, which also has a vowel quality 'like that of cardinal 4, [a]' (Wells, 1982: 305). We can therefore suggest that developments concerning this vowel in the two Southern Hemisphere varieties were independent events which happened in parallel, and that the same can be said for the development in London. These events were – and are – continuations of a long ongoing process of change involving the STRUT vowel, going back to the late 1500s, as we saw in Chapter 2.

NINETEENTH-CENTURY INNOVATIONS

I now turn to an examination of four cases of drift of the second type – that is, to forms which are present in modern Southern Hemisphere Englishes but which, I hypothesise, were not brought from the British Isles at all but rather developed in the early colonial varieties. I consider these changes to be more convincing examples of drift than the foregoing because, remarkably, all of them are to be found in modern Australian English, Falkland Islands English and, with one exception, in South African English, as well as in New

Zealand. I interpret this as an indication that the Southern Hemisphere varieties inherited propensities to these changes, rather than ongoing changes as such, from British Isles English. We can say with Andersen (2002: 21) that 'if an innovation is well motivated in one place, then it should be equally well motivated in other places'. The forty-year time depth present in the Mobile Unit Corpus, with the speakers analysed having birthdates ranging from 1850 to 1889, enables us furthermore to witness and demonstrate the first stages of these developments in New Zealand.

HAPPY Tensing

A very good example of such a change is presented by the phenomenon called by Wells (1982) HAPPY Tensing. This feature – the incidence of /iː/ rather than /ɪ/ in the final syllable of words such as *happy*, *money* – is the norm in modern New Zealand English. It was very rare in mid-nineteenth-century Britain but is currently very rapidly becoming the norm in England. At the level of regional accents in England, it is an innovation which appears to be most characteristic of southern accents. At the time of the settlement of New Zealand, it was confined to a rather small area in the English Southwest. Map 13 shows the extent of HAPPY Tensing in the SED materials and in modern dialects (Trudgill, 1999: 61; Wells, 1982: 380–6, Thomas, 1994: 120). The feature can be seen to have spread rather rapidly out of the English southwest in the space of a few generations. The presence of urban coastal areas in the north, such as Liverpool and Newcastle, with the newer form, indicates diffusion from one urban area to another, followed by subsequent spreading to surrounding rural areas. The relative newness of this phenomenon is something which is confirmed by the ONZE Project recordings: HAPPY Tensing is totally absent from the speech of our oldest informants. It then makes an appearance and subsequently increases. The percentage of speakers who have HAPPY Tensing by decade of birth in the ONZE Corpus is as follows:

1850–1859:	0%
1860–1869:	25%
1870–1879:	48%
1880–1889:	43%

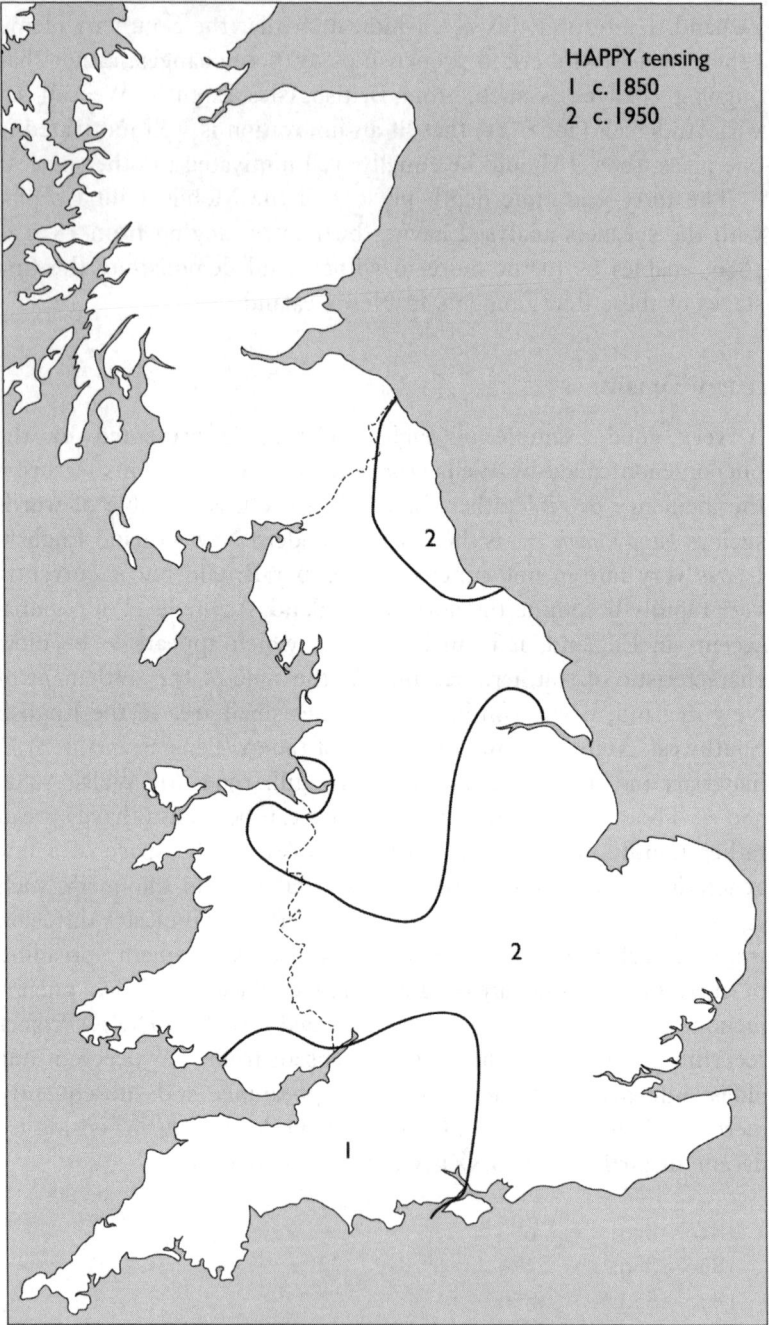

HAPPY tensing
1 c. 1850
2 c. 1950

2

2

1

Map 13: HAPPY Tensing

This chronological pattern suggests that HAPPY Tensing did not arrive in New Zealand from Britain at all but started life independently in New Zealand (although, of course, we accept that it might, in fact, have arrived from the English southwest at a level which fell below the crucial threshold for transmission). Then, as the figures show, it developed quite rapidly until, today, it has entirely taken over. New Zealand English has shared with southern, and increasingly northern, English English in the adoption of this feature in the last 150 years or so. This is another development in parallel which we can label drift. However, in this particular case, the striking thing is that we can see very clearly the kind of process discussed by Sapir in his treatment of umlauted plurals in the Germanic languages. New Zealand English did not inherit HAPPY Tensing. And it did not inherit an ongoing change as such. What it did inherit, apparently, was a propensity to replace /ɪ/ by /iː/. We assume that Australian English, South African English, Tristanian English and Falkland Islands English, which also have HAPPY Tensing (Wells, 1982: 595, 616), did the same. HAPPY Tensing also appears to be a relatively new feature in American English: Kenyon (1924, cited in Wells, 1982: 258) writes of it as being a feature of the speech of 'the younger generations'. We can suggest that this propensity lay in the fact that the distinction between /ɪ/ and /iː/ in English is neutralised in unstressed word-final position and that /ɪ/ can otherwise not occur in open syllables.

Glide Weakening

Another clear case which illustrates Sapir's thesis involves 'Glide Weakening', a term coined by Wells (1982: 614) and employed by him with reference to South African English. In my view, however, it is also extremely relevant to the description of New Zealand English, something which is confirmed by the transcriptions used by Bauer (1997: 389; and see also Watson et al., 1998), as well as to Australian English (see Bernard, 1989). Wells's term 'Diphthong Shift' refers to continuing processes, in recent stages of the Great Vowel Shift, whereby the rising diphthongs /iː, uː, ei, ou, ai, au/ are acquiring first elements which are increasingly removed from their second elements – for example, /au/ [ɐʊ > æʊ], /ai/ [aɪ > ɑɪ], and so on. Glide Weakening, although very little discussed in the

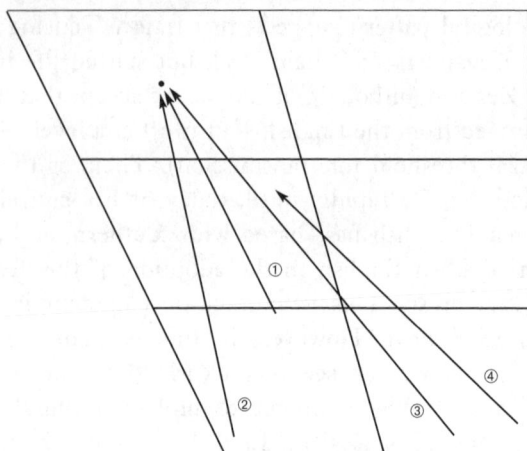

KEY: ① pre-RP   ② RP   ③ Diphthong Shift   ④ Glide Weakening

Figure 5: Diphthong Shift and Glide Weakening of /aɪ/

literature, would appear to be a continuation of this ongoing change. It is a kind of catching-up process whereby the second element of the diphthong compensates, as it were, for Diphthong Shift by moving to a position where it more closely approaches the first element, thereby once again reducing the distance between them – for example, /au/ [æʊ > æə], /ai/ [ɑi > ɑɛ] (see Figure 5). It is also often accompanied by a lengthening of the first element of the diphthong and a corresponding shortening of the second element – for example, /au/ [æə > æˑə].

Glide Weakening is a very distinctive feature of modern New Zealand English. It is also something which cannot to be regarded as being inherited from British Isles or other forms of English. It is true that some forms of Lancashire English and southern American English both have an /ai/ which is monophthongal or almost so. Other forms of northern English English have [aɛ] (Wells, 1982: 358). This, however, would not appear to be part of the same phenomenon since no prior Diphthong Shift has occurred in these cases – that is, the first element of the diphthong is (was) an unshifted [a]. More interesting is the well-known but now rather recessive monophthongal Cockney /au/ [æː]. Dialectal Cockney – but not London English in general – can also have a certain amount of Glide Weakening of /ai/ (Wells, 1982: 308). However, Glide Weakening applies much more extensively in New Zealand English and is most unlikely to derive solely from lower-working-class East End of London speech. I see it rather as a New Zealand innovation that ensued as a natural consequence of Diphthong Shift. That is, there was no actual inheritance from Britain of Glide Weakening as such but rather of a propensity to develop it in this form of colonial English.

The figures strengthen this assumption. The proportions of ONZE Project speakers who demonstrate Glide Weakening of at least one Diphthong Shifted vowel by decade of birth are as follows:

1850–1859	0%
1860–1869	44%
1870–1879	64%
1880–1889	57%

Once again, this looks very much like a New Zealand-based innovation. The important fact that it is also a feature of Australian English, and, crucially, of South African English and Falkland Islands English, confirms this drift-based hypothesis. Harrington et al. (1996) show very clear evidence of Glide Weakening in Australian English for FACE, GOAT, PRICE and MOUTH. For South Africa, Wells writes (1982: 614) that the PRICE vowel is subject to 'the weakening or loss of the second element of the diphthong' and that 'weakening of the second part of the diphthong is also characteristic of FACE, GOAT, CHOICE and MOUTH in some kinds of South African speech'. Falkland Islands English has Glide Weakening only for MOUTH and PRICE, and then only word-finally and before a voiced consonant – for example, [æˑʊ ~ aˑʊ] in *now*, *down* and [ɑˑɪ] in *buy*, *time*. (As we noted, Diphthong Shift has not occurred in pre-voiceless environments in the Falklands, and Glide Weakening would, therefore, not be expected.) Similarly, Tristan has Glide Weakening for the one vowel where it has Diphthong Shift, namely PRICE word-finally and before a voiced consonant.

None of these five colonial varieties, it seems, can have imported Glide Weakening from Britain as such. Neither can it be the case that one of them exported it to the other four: diffusion between Australia and New Zealand is, of course, conceivable, but diffusion to or from South Africa is not. Neither can it reasonably be thought to be the result in all five Southern Hemisphere cases of later, post-settlement diffusion from England, since English accents lag far behind in this development. Rather, what happened is that all five Southern Hemisphere Englishes inherited the same drift. The fact that Glide Weakening has not (yet) occurred to any great extent in Britain is something which demonstrates, as is always the case with linguistic change, that Diphthong Shift establishes a propensity to, but does not necessarily lead to, Glide Weakening. As we noted in Chapter 1, linguistic change is not deterministic to this extent!

The NURSE vowel

This vowel is a comparatively new one in English, and it occurs only in non-rhotic varieties. Its history is as follows. In Middle English there were three distinct vowels /ɪr/, /ɛr/ and /ʊr/ in contexts where the /r/ was non-prevocalic, as in *bird*, *earth*, *hurt*. These vowels underwent the First NURSE Merger (Wells, 1982: 200) in Early Modern English times, resulting in /ər/ in all three cases. Wells dates this merger to the sixteenth century, although Mac-Mahon suggests that it might have occurred later – which certainly was the case in some geographical areas of England (1994: 415–18). Next, Pre-R Lengthening took place in the seventeenth century (Wells, 1982: 201), with /ər/ becoming /əːr/. The quality of the vowel then became more open, to /ɜːr/. Later, R Dropping occurred (see above), resulting in /ɜː/. (None of this took place in Scotland, which still has the pronunciations /ɪr/, /ɛr/ and /ʊr/, as mentioned in Chapter 2. In some varieties of Irish English, /ɛr/ remains distinct while the merger has affected /ɪr/ and /ʊr/, resulting in /ər/.)

The RP-type vowel [ɜː], in *nurse*, *girl*, *bird*, etc., is actually not an especially common vowel in varieties of English around the world. For English English, the *Linguistic Atlas of England* shows very few areas which consistently have [ɜː] (written [əː]) in the relevant lexical set in 1950s–1960s Traditional-dialects – Cheshire, Staffordshire, Warwickshire, Northamptonshire, Huntingdonshire, Hertfordshire and Essex – and we can assume that, a hundred years earlier, this area would have been smaller. Wells (1982) states that Newcastle has [ɒ]; Liverpool, Middlesbrough, Hull, Coventry and a number of other places have [ɛ:], identical with the vowel of *there*; Birmingham has a raised [ɨ]. A number of Lancashire (Shorrocks, 1998) and southeast Welsh accents (Wells, 1982: 381) have a rounded [œ:] vowel which the SED materials also show for Monmouthshire. East Anglian English had /aː/ in open syllables and in closed syllables that were derived from original /ɛr/; and /ɐ/ in other closed syllables until the mid-twentieth century: *her* /haː/, *learn* /laːnt/, *bird* /bɐd/ (Trudgill, 1997). For varieties outside of the British Isles, Tristan da Cunha has a system which resembles the East Anglian system (Schreier and Trudgill, forthcoming), but the /aː/ which occurs in *her, learnt* is not the same vowel as the /ɑː/ which occurs in START, and *bird* has the STRUT vowel, which also occurs, remarkably, in open syllables in words not derived from older /ɛr/, as in *fur* /fʌ/. Some forms of Caribbean English have NURSE as [ɔ]; and some non-rhotic American accents, such as New York City and New Orleans, have the diphthong [ɜɪ] in NURSE.

Given that the RP-type vowel [ɜ:] is actually a rather uncommon vowel in varieties of English, it is perhaps not surprising that New Zealand English also has a NURSE vowel which is rather different from RP. The modern New Zealand English variant (with the exception of Southland where constriction survives and may even be on the increase – Bartlett, 2003) is typically fronted and raised compared to English English and is also lip-rounded [ø: – œ: – ɵ:]. It is my contention that this, too, is a nineteenth-century New Zealand innovation. The figures by decade of birth for the ONZE Project informants who have lip-rounding of NURSE are as follows:

1850–1859	0%
1860–1869	16%
1870–1879	28%
1880–1889	43%

Of great importance here is the rather remarkable fact that Australian English (Bradley and Bradley, 1979: 68; Turner, 1994: 292), South African English (Wells, 1982: 615; Branford, 1994: 481), and Falkland Islands English (Sudbury, 2000) all also have fronted, raised and rounded vowels in NURSE. We cannot use British antecedents as an explanation for this development. It is true that certain Lancashire and southeast Welsh accents also have a front rounded vowel, but the accents of these areas would have been far too much in the minority in the Southern Hemisphere mixtures to have had any influence in the new dialects. Only 1% of immigrants to New Zealand, up to 1881, came from any part of Wales (Mc-Kinnon, 1997), and Lancashire did not figure prominently, either. And, once again, we would not want to entertain an explanation involving diffusion from one of the four Southern Hemisphere varieties to the other three.

The coincidence of this feature developing in four Southern Hemisphere varieties is clearly an instance of drift. And we can go some considerable way to explaining where the propensity to this drift lay. (I owe this explanation to Margaret Maclagan.) There is a clear relationship between the new vowel quality and loss of rhoticity. The new, rounded vowel occurs only in non-rhotic dialects. Early New Zealand English was predominantly rhotic, and so we would not expect it to have any rounded vowels in this lexical set, especially since even accents which are only vestigially rhotic maintain /r/ longest and most frequently in NURSE words. Clearly the new vowel quality could not have developed until the loss of rhoticity had taken place, which was well after the arrival of anglophones in New Zealand. Certainly we have heard no tokens on the ONZE tapes which are both rhotacised and lip-rounded.

This relationship between loss of rhoticity and the development of rounded /ɜ:/ appears to be a causal one. There is a very straightforward acoustic explanation for why loss of rhoticity might be compensated for by the development of lip-rounding. The most salient acoustic effect of rhoticity is the lowering of the third formant frequency of a vowel, combined with some lowering of the second formant. Lip-rounding also has the effect of lowering all formant frequencies – though not as dramatically as rhoticity for formant three (Kent and Read, 1992). Thus, as rhoticity was lost, lip-rounding largely compensated for the loss of /r/ and preserved the formant structure of the NURSE vowel.

LATER INNOVATIONS

The Second FORCE Merger

The Second FORCE Merger represents another example of drift which probably postdates the new-dialect formation process of the Southern Hemisphere Englishes. The merger, which is 'now under way' (Wells, 1982: 237), is leading to the lowering and mono-phthongisation of the /ʊə/ of *poor, cure* from [ʊə] to [oə] and, via [ɔə], to [ɔ:], so that *poor, pore* and *paw* are now all homophonous. The ongoing status of this change suggests that it could not have been part of the mid-nineteenth-century British input to New Zealand English. It is, however, fully established in Tristanian English, and is currently underway in New Zealand English, as well as in Australian English (see Wells, 1982: 599, 609) and Falkland Islands English (Andrea Sudbury, p.c.). It appears, however, to be absent, so far, from South African English which, on the other hand, along with Falkland Islands English and the English of southeastern England, notably London, is experiencing the movement of the NORTH–FORCE–THOUGHT vowel upwards from [ɔ:] to [o:] or, in Tristanian, [oə].

The NEAR–SQUARE Merger

There is also a further possible candidate for the label of drift in Southern Hemisphere Englishes. It also clearly postdates the new-dialect formation process but is of interest because, like the Second FORCE Merger, it points to the fact that drift-type developments may occur even many generations after separation. We saw, very briefly above, that modern New Zealand English is characterised by the merger of vowels from the lexical sets of NEAR and SQUARE. This is a recent feature which clearly developed during the twentieth century, well after the formation of New Zealand English (Mac-lagan and Gordon, 1996). The single vowel resulting from the merger can be either a monophthong or a centring diphthong, with the most common realisation perhaps being intermediate in quality between the two original vowels, around [e̞:(ə) ~ ɪ:(ə)]. Margaret Maclagan (p.c.) points to the parallel in New Zealand English between the historical raising of the DRESS vowel and the raising of

SQUARE, and indeed the first element of the NEAR/SQUARE vowel does appear to be identical with the DRESS vowel for very many New Zealand speakers. The merger is now soldily established, and can be seen in punning advertisements such as *Hair it is!* for a hairdressing salon.

The merger is not found in Australian or South African English. It is found, however, in the English of Tristan da Cunha (see Schreier, 2003: 210), as well as in the English of St Helena, in both cases on [ɪʲə]. And it is quite possibly to be found in the English of the Falkland Islands. Sudbury (2000) discusses this issue and, although she carefully avoids saying that a merger has occurred, she does suggest that it may have occurred for some speakers or be in the process of doing so. My own analyses show that the Falkland Islands SQUARE vowel is very different from that encountered in most areas of Britain. The distinctive Falklands vowel is a close monophthong, around [ẹː ~ eː], which contrasts strongly with the typical English English [ɛː(ə)] and which brings it very close, to say the least, to NEAR which may also be monophthongal.

The structural predisposition for this change to take place is presumably the low functional load of these two vowels and their phonetic similarity: Fry (1947) showed that the two vowels are very infrequent and, between them, account for only 0.55% of phoneme tokens in English. Note also the parallel between the merger of these front vowels and the Second FORCE Merger which is occurring in the back vowels (see above). A similar merger of NEAR and SQUARE has occurred in East Anglia, but here the phonetic details are different, the merger being on [ɛː]; and in parts of the Caribbean, such as Montserrat, where it is on [ɪɐ] (Wells, 1982: 587); as well as in Newfoundland.

The short front vowels again

I argued in Chapter 2 that the difference in quality between the vowels of KIT, DRESS, TRAP in England and the Southern Hemisphere was due not to a raising of these vowels to a closer position in the Southern Hemisphere (although I conceded that this has, in fact, happened in more recent times in New Zealand English) but to a lowering of these vowels to a more open position in the English of England. One of my arguments in favour of this approach was that it was more reasonable to conceive of lowering happening once – in England – than raising happening on four separate occasions in four separate places – Australia, New Zealand, the Falklands and South Africa. Now that we have addressed the issue of parallel developments, however, this seems to be a less powerful argument: clearly, if the fronting and rounding of NURSE can occur in the Southern Hemisphere Englishes separately and without it happening in England, then we have to concede that the same thing could have happened with the short front vowels also. However, the evidence is against this, in that we do also genuinely have evidence for the lowering of these vowels in English English, as I showed earlier: recall, to cite just one example, that Wells (1982: 129) wrote of the TRAP vowel in England that 'it is a striking fact that the current trend in pronunciation of this vowel is ... towards an opener [a]-like' quality. I therefore see no need to revise the analysis given earlier.

CHAPTER 7

Determinism and social factors

In this book I have (mostly) implicitly made a sociolinguistic point which I now make totally explicit. I have argued that the new-dialect formation which resulted from the mixture of dialects brought from the British Isles to New Zealand (and the other Southern Hemisphere colonies) was not a haphazard process but, on the contrary, deterministic in nature. This entails that what happened was, for any given feature and allowing for unmarking, that the minority quite simply and mechanistically accommodated to the majority. In other words, like Britain (forthcoming), I do not find it at all necessary, in considering Stages II and III of new-dialect formation in tabula rasa situations, to call on the social factor of 'prestige' or related factors such as 'status' and 'stigma' as explanatory factors. Nor do I invoke 'identity' or 'ideology' as factors that were involved.

PATTERNS OF INTERACTION

I prefer, rather, to follow Labov's view that patterns of interaction, of the type I have already alluded to in Chapters 3 and 4, should always be consulted for possible explanations before one jumps to conclusions about identity and prestige. Labov's main preoccupation is with the diffusion of linguistic forms but, in my view, new-dialect formation, which depends just as much as diffusion on how individual speakers behave linguistically in face-to-face interaction, can be regarded in precisely the same way. Labov argues that 'as always, it is good practice to consider first the simpler and more mechanical view that social structure affects linguistic output through changes in frequency of interaction' (Labov, 2001: 506). Bloomfield asserts (1933: 476), in a statement that tacitly accepts the point I made earlier about the innate human tendency to adjust our behaviour to that of those we associate with, that

> every speaker is constantly adapting his speech-habits to those of his interlocutors ... The inhabitants of a settlement ... talk much more to each other than to persons who live elsewhere. When any innovation in the way of speaking spreads over a district, the limit of this spread is sure to be along some lines of weakness in the network of oral communication.

Labov argues that it follows from this that 'a large part of the problem of explaining the diffusion of linguistic change is reduced to a simple calculation' (2001: 19). It is purely a matter of who interacts most often with who – a matter of density of communication. I have argued above that levelling is equally a matter of simple calculation.

Labov then develops the *principle of density* as follows:

> The principle of density implicitly asserts that we do not have to search for a motivating force behind the diffusion of linguistic change. The effect is mechanical and inevitable; the implicit assumption is that social evaluation and attitudes play a minor role. (2001: 20)

This holds just as well for new-dialect formation, which is equally mechanical and inevitable, as we have seen.

Opponents of this view might want to argue for the relevance of social factors in the formation of New Zealand English by pointing, for example, to the fact that, on the ONZE Project tapes, there is a tendency for male speakers to use more nonstandard forms than female speakers. Given that we know from very many other studies in long-established communities that female speakers tend on average to favour prestige forms to a greater extent than male speakers, this would seem to provide evidence that prestige might have been involved at Stage II of the new-dialect formation process. Of course, this tendency on the tapes could be the result of the same sort of methodological problem mentioned before, namely that the elderly male speakers have been less affected, during the course of their long lifetimes, by twentieth-century notions of correctness and prestige than the women. But, if it is not, I would still prefer to explain it purely and simply in terms of patterns of interaction. If women at Stage I brought more standard forms with them from Britain than men did, then the speech of small girls at Stage II may on average reflect this fact as a result of a greater frequency of interaction with older women than with older men. Labov (2001: 191) says of linguistic changes that they 'may simply reflect changes in interlocutor frequencies'. I would say the same thing for differences in acquired linguistic characteristics also, namely that they, too, simply reflect differences in interlocutor frequencies

It seems to me that what we witness, in the new-dialect formation process associated with tabula rasa colonial situations, is what Croft terms a 'nonintentional mechanism for selection'. In Croft's evolutionary approach to language change, he distinguishes between a number of causal mechanisms. The *mechanism for normal replication* 'involves simple replication of the existing structure, thereby extending its lineage' (2000: 73). *Mechanisms of altered replication* 'create novel variants that did not already exist in that lineage'. And *mechanisms of selection* are those 'that favor a particular form being adopted among members of a speech community' and require 'previously created variants to operate on, choosing one over another'. This can, of course, happen in any speech community. What is different about a tabula rasa colonial dialect contact situation is that selection has to happen on a massive scale; in the formation of the Southern Hemisphere Englishes, all the vowels and many of the consonants presented different varaints, and there was considerable grammatical and lexical variation as well.

According to Croft, mechanisms can also be *intentional* or *nonintentional*. Intentional mechanisms are those 'that are not teleological but involve the intention of a speaker to achieve some other goal in language use' and which 'give rise to what Keller (1994: 57) calls phenomena of the third kind: an unintended result of an intended action' (Croft, 2000: 65). Such intentional selectional mechanisms would include those involving factors such as prestige.

On the other hand,

> reinforcement and decay of entrenchment represent a non-intentional mechanism for selection. If a speaker replicates one form instead of another *as a function of exposure to use (measured for example by token frequency)* [...] then differential replication has occurred independent of any intentional goal of the speaker. In fact differential replication may occur despite any intentional goal of the speaker. (Croft, 2000: 74, my italics)

Importantly, Croft also argues, in an echo of the point made by Labov cited above, that in looking for explanatory mechanisms for change '(barring direct evidence to the contrary) a good methodological strategy would be to seek nonintentional mechanisms first, and only turn to intentional mechanisms if those fail' (2000: 78).

PRESTIGE

Advocates for the importance of the role of prestige might want to point out that, in our discussion of reallocation, we noted the example of Australian English which has retained – and reallocated – two different pronunciations of the set of *dance*, with the /aː/ vowel being associated with rather more prestigious varieties, and /æ/ with lower-status varieties. This might be interpreted as indicating a role for social factors in the formation of Australian English. In actual fact, however, Turner points out (1994: 293) that, although there is in modern times some social differentiation here (Bradley, 1991), the real difference of distribution in contemporary Australia is regional: /aː/ is usual in Adelaide, and /æ/ in Sydney (Horvath and Horvath, 1989). Crucially, Turner also shows that, in the earlier years of the Australian colony, any social connotations associated with these two variants were actually the other way around (1994: 294), which is not surprising when it is considered that the /aː/ vowel in this set was originally a lower-class innovation in England; we saw above that MacMahon (1994: 456) argued that the change started amongst 'the lower sections of society'. We can assume, then, that the acquisition of any different status connotations for the two variants postdated the formation of Australian English.

Advocates for the role of prestige might also want to argue that what I have referred to as drift is really nothing more than the result of continuing influence from prestigious metropolitan English English. 'Continued influence' is, after all, a phenomenon which we know to occur in colonial situations. For example, it is widely, though not universally, agreed that the loss of non-prevocalic /r/, as an innovation in English, spread from London to those locations on the east coast of the United States which were in closest contact with southern England: Boston, Massachusetts; New York City; Richmond, Virginia; Charleston, South Carolina; and Savannah, Georgia (see Kurath, 1964: 148; Ash, 1999). Similarly, Lipski (1994: 51) says that Latin American Spanish, having arrived in the Americas in the early 1500s, 'remained sensitive to linguistic developments in Spain up to the end of the seventeenth century i.e. for about 200 years'. I acknowledge this possibility for New Zealand, and especially for the Falkland Islands. However, it is most unlikely in those cases where developments have gone further in the Southern Hemisphere Englishes than in England, as with STRUT Fronting and Diphthong Shift, that this can work as an explanation. And it certainly does not apply where developments have taken place in the Southern Hemisphere which have not occurrred at all in English English, such as the rounding and fronting of the vowel of NURSE and Glide Weakening. Moroever, it is clear that Lipksi is commenting on a lengthy period well *after* the initial formation of Latin American Spanish, and that the American English development also postdates the actual formation of that colonial variety or varieties – witness the fact that non-prevocalic /r/ loss affected only coastal areas. The importation of rhoticity loss to the United States occurred *after* the formation of a focussed, stable variety there, by which time prestige would once again have kicked in as a relevant factor.

I would therefore reject any suggestion that the development of non-rhoticity in New Zealand had anything to do with the importation of a British prestige-based innovation *during* its formation period. Such a thesis would also be inconsistent with the fact that, in all other respects, New Zealand English most certainly has not followed English English as a prestige model. No other prestige feature – GOAT Fronting (see Wells, 1982), for instance – has been introduced into New Zealand English from Britain, and indeed all the developments that have taken place in New Zealand English have been *away* from the external British prestige RP norm, not towards it. The accelerated (as compared to England) development of Diphthong Shift, the rapid fronting of STRUT, the rounding of the vowel in NURSE, and the other developments that have occurred subsequently can none of them be ascribed to the prestige influence of English English.

It should also be said that prestige is, in any case, not an especially helpful notion anyway. As Labov has argued, its apparently explanatory force is

> considerably weakened if the term 'prestige' is allowed to apply to any property of a linguistic trait that would lead people to imitate it. Thus the fact that a linguistic form has prestige would be shown by the fact that it was adopted by others. (2001: 24)

It is also a notion whose operation we can have little idea about in the early years of a newly developing colonial society. I suggest, in fact, that, in a situation of the tabula rasa colonial new-dialect formation type, social factors such as prestige (and including 'covert prestige' – Trudgill, 1972) have no role to play except amongst adults at Stage I.

STIGMA

Proponents for the importance of the role of social features might also want to point to the other side of the coin of prestige, social stigma, as an important factor in determining the final form of colonial varieties. For example, they might want to suggest that H Dropping disappeared from New Zealand English not because it was a minority feature but as a result of normative pressure from schoolteachers and others against a low-prestige pronunciation which has, from time to time and in certain places and by some people, been highly overtly stigmatised. I would also reject this argument.

It is true that, in Trudgill (1986a), I suggested that a crucial mechanism in new-dialect formation was accommodation in face-to-face interaction, as we have noted above; that I argued there that one of the key factors in controlling accommodation was salience –

speakers accommodate to features which they notice; and that one of the features that may produce salience is the fact that 'greater awareness attaches to forms which are overtly stigmatised' where 'there is a high status variant of the stigmatised form *and* this high status variant tallies with the orthography while the stigmatised variant does not' (p. 11). In this book, I have in any case argued that salience cannot be operative in tabula rasa colonial situations where young children do not yet have established phonologies, but I would further point out here that this particular source of salience cannot be relevant in the case of pre-literate (or illiterate – see below) children. The notion of stigma would also be a dangerous one to use in a colonial situation where contact with the prestige norms of the mother country had been weakened.

We can assume that in the early colonial period most people (I am not saying 'all') had better things to do with their lives than worry about whether they 'dropped their *h*s' or not. Just as the sorts of prescriptivists who write complaining letters to the newspapers today are atypical, small in number and totally without influence, so we can assume that they had a comparable and probably even bigger lack of influence in nineteenth-century New Zealand also. Indeed, in early New Zealand, no mechanisms were in place for the effective dissemination of prescriptive views to the mass of the community (Britain, forthcoming). There was no compulsory schooling in New Zealand until 1877, for instance, and the illiteracy rate in 1858 was 25% (Belich, 1996: 393). And, even if there had been such mechanisms, there is no reason to believe that anyone would have paid any attention, any more and indeed probably rather less than they do anywhere else. According to Belich (1996: 330) 'for European settlers migration was a chance to select cultural baggage – to discard as well as take. Highly overt class differences, excessive deference towards the upper classes, and customs that publicly implied subordination were leading candidates for the discard pile.'

We cannot help but observe, moreover, that H Dropping today is alive, and very well, and still spreading, in England and Wales, in spite of centuries of normative pressure. And it can be argued that one explanation for why Diphthong Shift and Glide Weakening have progressed more rapidly in New Zealand than in England is precisely that these developments have been unrestrained by the effective presence of prescriptive attitudes and by contact with, and thus the influence of, RP in the new colonial situation. Wells (1982: 593) makes this point explicitly:

> All southern hemisphere English … carries forward trends already present in popular accents in the south-east of England in the early nineteenth century, but enabled to develop more rapidly and thoroughly as a consequence of their being freed from the omnipresent restraining influence of RP. In a village or small town of, say, Bedfordshire in 1800, a man would be in regular contact with RP speakers (squire, rector, doctor), and the social pressures to admire and imitate qualities associated with this culturally dominant social class were strong … But someone transported to an antipodean penal settlement, or migrating independently to seek a new life in a far country, thereby cut himself free both from the hierarchical pressures of English social stratification and from regular contact with RP speakers.

This lack of contact with RP, moreover, would have begun as soon as emigrants set foot on board ship. Daniel Schreier (p.c.) has pointed out that, even on the voyage out to the colonies, accommodation segregated by class would have meant that there was little contact between upper-class RP speakers and others.

And if the picture Wells paints was true for the adults, how much truer it must have been for children. I have argued above that the work of new-dialect formation at the second and third stages in New Zealand was clearly carried out by young children, who would have been more or less impervious to prestige norms, if indeed there were any such norms. Children do not speak like their school-teachers (Trudgill, 1975); and as already mentioned in Chapter 2, the conventional sociolinguistic wisdom is that children speak like their peers. Following McWhorter (2000), we can agree that arguments from normative pressure are

> sociolinguistically very implausible. Sociolinguistics has taught us that vernacular dialects tend to be hardy in competition with dominant standards, and that it takes a great deal more than mere exposure to standard dialects in school to eliminate them from a speech community.

Much more usually, features spread *from* low-status lects *to* prestige varieties, not the other way round – witness the spread of T Glottalling into British RP (Trudgill, 2002), the spreading of the back variant of /a:/ into RP, the change from /æ/ to /a:/ in *dance*, etc., and the loss of rhoticity in England. However, it is not necessary to invoke attitudinal factors such as 'covert prestige' for this sort of phenomenon either. The density principle will work just as well – RP speakers in Britain have always been extremely heavily outnumbered by speakers with non-RP accents.

Once again, however, I prefer to let the linguistic data speak for themselves. There is no evidence that features for which low prestige might be held to be important were actually stigmatised by the New Zealand-bound emigrants themselves, either before they left Britain or in early colonial New Zealand. We have considerable amounts of H Dropping on the ONZE Project recordings. And stigmatised and much criticised low-status forms, such as Diphthong Shift, have shown no signs of being reversed as a result of normative pressure in New Zealand or anywhere else. If stigma or prestige had played a role, randomness and patterns of interaction would not have been so influential in the development of the idiolects of the first generation of New-Zealand-born anglophones – the ONZE Project informants, and British lower-class dialects would have contributed little or nothing to the English of the second generation. Of course, from 1890 onwards, social factors may have begun to play a role – but my claim is that *they were not relevant in the actual new-dialect formation process itself*: New Zealand English in 1900 did not, for instance, have Diphthong Shift because this was prestigious; and it did not have front /a:/ because this had high social status.

IDENTITY AND IDEOLOGY

Also in this book I have not had to have recourse to the notion of 'identity' (or to related factors such as 'ideology'). It is as well to be sceptical about 'identity' as a factor in linguistic change generally. Labov's famous Martha's Vineyard study (1963) is often cited as an uncontroversial example of the important role of identity. Labov himself, however, is not so sure. He writes (2001: 191):

The Martha's Vineyard study is frequently cited as a demonstration of the importance of the concept of local identity in the motivation of linguistic change. However, we do not often find correlations between degrees of local identification and the progress of sound change.

And it is clear that identity factors cannot lead to the *development* of new linguistic features. It would be ludicrous to suggest that New Zealand English speakers deliberately developed, say, closer front vowels in order to symbolise some kind of local or national New Zealand identity.

This is, of course, not necessarily the same thing as saying that, once new linguistic features have developed, they cannot *become* emblematic, although it is as well to be sceptical about the extent to which this sort of phenomenon does actually occur also. For example, we can say that the twentieth-century innovation in New Zealand English whereby the KIT vowel became centralised might perhaps now constitute a symbol of New Zealand identity and that the vowel might for that reason in future even become more centralised. But I have to say that I would, personally, find even this unconvincing. Why do New Zealanders need to symbolise their identity as New Zealanders when most of them spend most of their time, as is entirely normal, talking to other New Zealanders? But in any case we most certainly cannot argue that New Zealanders deliberately centralised this vowel *in order to* develop an identity marker.

It is also deeply improbable that the children who were responsible for the mixture out of which New Zealand English later grew – including the children who subsequently became the ONZE Project informants – were symbolising individual mixed identities by means of their individual mixed idiolects. It is also equally unlikely that the children who in the third generation led the levelling and focussing that gave rise to New Zealand English proper were motivated by any prestige or identity-based factors in their selection of (from an English English perspective) upper-class H Retention, lower-class Diphthong Shift, urban non-rhoticity, and the rural Weak Vowel Merger, from among all the features that were available to them.

THE NEW-DIALECT FORMATION SCENARIO

I therefore suggest that the evidence available to us indicates the following deterministic scenario for the initial development of New Zealand English and thus, very probably, of the other colonial varieties also. The parents of the first significant generation of New Zealand-born English speakers were born (mostly) in Britain, in the years around and after 1815, and acquired the English dialects of that time and of their native localities. These were the forms of English that were taken to New Zealand from about 1840 onwards (Stage I). These forms of English must have included rural Traditional-dialects, but Traditional-dialect forms are rare, as we saw in Chapter 3, on the Mobile Unit tapes, suggesting that they were for the most part levelled out – the process I have called 'rudimentary levelling' – by the adult British emigrants on the boat or soon after arrival as a result of accommodation in face-to-face interaction. These same adult speakers, too, would have been responsible for the development of *interdialect* phenomena. Interdialect phenomena of the *intermediate form* type can be ascribed to *partial* accommodation. Interdialect phenomena of the *hyperadaptation* type, on the other hand, can be ascribed to *imperfect* accommodation, and would have been particularly associated with adult and therefore less-than-expert language learners. Insofar as hyperadaptation took the form of hypercorrection – attempting to employ more statusful forms than one normally uses – this would also indicate a role for normative attitudes. Note that it is only at Stages II and III that I am arguing for a total absence of social factors.

For the (Stage II) children born in New Zealand from 1840 onwards, however, the situation would have been very different. For them there was no single peer-group dialect to accommodate to as there usually is for children arriving in a new location. Rather, all of them, except those who lived in the most isolated of settlements, were surrounded by an enormously variable set of models consisting of dialects from all over the British Isles. Even many decades later, the speech of these people, as elderly adults on the ONZE Project tapes, demonstrates that, since there was no particular reason to select one vowel or consonant or grammatical variant rather than another, children were free to choose (although I am not suggesting at all that any conscious decision was involved). They were certainly not responsive to, and therefore not motivated by, notions of prestige or stigma – as is clear from the fact that they all selected different combinations.

Patterns of interaction would have been important here: for any individual child, people he or she interacted with most would have had more chance of influencing the final form of the child's speech than those who did not. But we should also not exclude the possibility that chance played a role – McWhorter (2000: 77) writes of 'the vital role chance plays in language contact'. The picture I portrayed above was of young children randomly selecting some forms here and some forms there as if in a supermarket. This absence of a single model dialect led to a situation where children acquired dialects that were very variable, that differed from one another even if they grew up together, and that consisted for the most part of forms derived from British dialects but in original combinations not found anywhere in the British Isles.

It is chastening for linguists, moreover, to see that systematicity seems to have played a very small role here. That is, these children do genuinely seem to have acquired linguistic forms on an individual, feature-by-feature basis. One would have supposed, for example, that speakers with an open TRAP vowel, say, would also necessarily have had an open DRESS vowel; or that speakers with H Dropping would also necessarily have had the /hw/–/w/ Merger – but this is not so.

However, I have also pointed out that, though chance was involved in the development of individual idiolects in this first generation of the New-Zealand-born (Stage II), the proportions of variants found in their idiolects *collectively* is not random at all but reflects the proportions of such variants in the dialect mixture around them. This is the randomness and transmission point discussed in Chapter 5.

At this second stage, accommodation did not play any significant role. I do not mean to suggest that accommodation did not take place at all but, obviously, children did not accommodate to one another in any *systematic* way – or children in the same family and in the same settlement would not have ended up with radically different idiolects. We do see, however, the results of a phenomenon which resembles levelling but which I have labelled 'apparent levelling' because accommodation was not involved. That is, children would not have acquired features, however widespread they were back in Britain, which were present in the mixture with frequencies of occurrence below a certain threshold level. This is why a number of mainstream features very common in British accents and dialects did not make it into the speech of the ONZE Project informants.

Finally, at Stage III, in the second New Zealand-born generation, starting with those born in about 1865 and reaching a culmination in the speech of those born by 1890, we see the actual first appearance of New Zealand English as such. That is, by about 1905, adolescents, at least, would have been speaking a distinctively New Zealand form of English.

This was the result of a *focussing* process which led to a stable dialect and which completed the process of *new-dialect formation*. This focussing was preceded by *koinéisation*, which consisted of *levelling, unmarking* and *reallocation*, as discussed in Chapter 5. Of particular interest are the processes of levelling and unmarking. I have argued that the mechanism by means of which the many individual variants present in early settlements in New Zealand were reduced via accommodation to a single variant was deterministic in nature. In nearly all cases, the feature which was in the majority in the mixture spoken by the first generation of New Zealand-born speakers was the one to survive in the speech of the second generation. (I also noted, especially in connection with H Dropping, that the phrase 'in the majority' can mean 'present in the speech of a majority of speakers' but also, for variable features, 'the most commonly occurring variant in terms of tokens'.) The only exceptions are cases where a large minority variant survives because it had the linguistic advantage of being unmarked or simpler than a small majority variant; or where (Samuels, 1972: 108) a minority form is conveniently intermediate between other forms in the mixture of roughly equivalent strength, and can act as a compromise. Certainly, it was not the case that variants survived because they were prestigious – or New Zealand English would be phonetically much closer to RP than it is!

UNIFORMITY

By the beginning of the twentieth century, then, a relatively uniform variety of New Zealand English would have been in place. I

DETERMINISM AND SOCIAL FACTORS

say 'relatively' because there is, even today, no total geographical uniformity, and the jury has still to be out on whether such uniformity will decrease or increase. Social uniformity, moreover, has certainly not been achieved either, and there are incontrovertibly some social class differences in modern New Zealand English, though many fewer than in Britain.

Nevertheless, this uniformity does need to be explained. I have accounted for the distinctive nature of New Zealand English and its relative uniformity in terms of its growth out of a mixture of British dialects, plus the deterministic nature of the new-dialect formation process – Chapter 1 quotes Bernard (1981) as saying that 'the ingredients of the mixing bowl were very much the same, and at different times and in different places the same process was carried out and the same end point achieved'. And yet it is probable that the *precise* nature of the mixture would have varied, at least somewhat, from one individual settlement to another. (We have already noted that this is how the rather distinctive nature of Southland English is to be accounted for.) The same problem arises for Australian English, which has an astonishing degree of geographical uniformity for so large a country. One explanatory factor for this uniformity has to be the drift which we discussed in the Chapter 6. As Wells (1982: 594) suggests, trends present in nineteenth-century English were carried forward more rapidly in Australia and New Zealand than in Britain 'which would have had the consequence of sharply reducing the social variability of speech in the new colonies'.

Another clue comes from a comparison. Contrast what happened in Australasia with the rather different consequences of dialect contact in sixteenth-century Spanish America: 'in each town and city of the New World, a slightly different dialect mixture came about, as a result of the different geographical and social origins of the settlers' (Penny 2000: 146). This was new-dialect formation at a period in history with rather slower transportation possibilities, in an enormous area, much of it with very difficult terrain, and with much less mobility. We are therefore inclined to agree with Bernard (1969) who argues, in the case of Australia, for geographical mobility and the fact that Australians in different parts of the country kept in touch with one another, mainly though sea travel from one port to another, as accounting for the uniformity.

For nineteenth-century New Zealand, Britain (forthcoming)

similarly cites high levels of mobility and transience, and suggests that these factors 'led to the emergence of an atomistic society freeing people both from subservience and from the need to conform that tight-knit local communities often engender'. According to Belich (1996: 414), between half and three-quarters of all New Zealand households in the mid-nineteenth century had moved on fifteen years later. As Britain points out, this was thus a society with relatively weak social network ties – precisely the sorts of ties that are the breeding ground for rapid supralocal linguistic change.

I would also add diffusion as an explanation. Just as I have suggested in my discussion of drift that linguistic change would have continued in the usual way during the new-dialect formation period, so the geographical diffusion of linguistic innovations from one place to another would also have continued in the normal way and would have helped, aided by high mobility, to strengthen the reduction of geographical and social differences.

COMPLICATIONS

We have noted that my three-stage scenario is not the whole story. Certain features present in early New Zealand English represent continuations of changes already in progress in England and/or in some way inherited from there. The four Southern Hemisphere varieties of English – Australian, New Zealand, Falkland Island and South African – not only inherited the results of the changes that had occurred so far in England but also continued them after separation. I have presented evidence to show that certain similarities between these geographically separated varieties are due, not to contact between them or to shared inherited features as such, but to the fact that, having derived from some common source, they continued to evolve linguistically, in similar directions, as a result of *drift* even after separation. There was a dynamism inherent in these ongoing changes which led to them continuing in parallel in the four different locations, although not always at the same speed and not always coinciding in absolutely all details. However, the most striking instances of drift that we noted involved features which were not present at all as such in British Isles English before the immigration to the main anglophone Southern Hemisphere colonies took place, and which subsequently evolved independently in all four of them. In these cases, we have to say that drift involves propensities to linguistic changes resulting from structural properties which varieties inherit. The inheritance is of structural conditions which at a later date may, but need not, lead to the development of new but identical or very similar linguistic changes in different varieties with a common ancestry.

The Founder Effect

And there is a further respect in which the three stages which I have described in Chapters 3, 4 and 5 represent an idealisation of what actually happened. Inevitably, things were very much more untidy than that. Immigration continued throughout the period under review, and the different stages will have overlapped to a considerable extent until focussing was complete and some kind of 'founder effect' took over. Mufwene (1991), borrowing a well-known term from biology (see Dobzhansky, 1963; Harrison et al., 1988), has adapted the term 'founder principle' to sociohistorical linguistics. As Mufwene points out (2001: 28), this principle is very similar to what Zelinsky (1973) has termed the 'doctrine of first effective settlement', and to Sankoff's (1980) 'first past the post principle'. Put simply, the founder effect implies that the linguistic founding population of an area has a built-in advantage when it comes to the continuing influence and survival of their speech forms, as opposed to those of later arrivals. It has often been pointed out, for example, that there are in the USA today more people who are descended from native German speakers than there are people who are descended from native English speakers. From the point of view of Labov's density principle, we can interpret what happened, mechanistically, as follows: the USA is an English-speaking country today because English speakers arrived first, and at any given time German-speaking immigrants who arrived later and, as it were, in dribs and drabs over a rather lengthy period were not sufficiently numerous for English to be replaced. This principle is implicitly recognised by Lipski (1994: 22), who says, for Latin American Spanish, that:

> when the bearers of the latest linguistic fashions in Spain were significantly outnumbered by an already flourishing speech

community, the impact of the innovation would be minimal, but when the founding of a major settlement was carried out by a group of new arrivals from Spain, the seminal effects of the first settlers might be sufficient to leave a lasting imprint on the developing regional dialect for generations to come.

Similarly, Poirier (1994: 257) claims for Canadian French that 'the first groups of colonists had a particular influence in the process of linguistic unification' (my translation).

Of course, as Mufwene concedes (2001: 76), the founder principle works unless it doesn't. In terms of Labov's principle, we can envisage situations where newcomers, demographically and therefore ultimately linguistically, totally overwhelm those who arrived first. Indeed, we can actually see this in the history of New Zealand English – the 'founders' were not those who arrived in 1800 but the large groups of migrants who arrived in the initial period from 1840 onwards. Lipski (1994: 54) similarly points out for colonial Spanish that:

> when one considers that a typical fleet arriving at Cartagena, Portobelo or Lima might bring several hundred settlers, the possible linguistic effects of a contingent of new settlers on an evolving dialect could be considerable. A single fleet could, under some circumstances, bring new arrivals who amounted to nearly half the resident population, and even if not all new settlers remained in the port of entry, their linguistic contributions would not be inconsequential.

CONCLUSION

The initial shape of New Zealand English, and thus by implication of the other colonial varieties, can be accounted for, then, in terms of the mixing together of different dialects of English from the British Isles, plus drift. The ONZE Project data set, unique in the study of the development of new varieties of English and providing data from large numbers of speakers, together with theoretical insights from the study of new-dialect formation arrived at independently before work on New Zealand English began, enable us to build up a rather detailed picture of the early development of new colonial varieties of English.

I have shown that dialect mixture and new-dialect formation are not haphazard processes; and that similarities between different geographically separated varieties, such as the transplanted Englishes of the Southern Hemisphere, can therefore be due to the fact that they have resulted from mixtures of similar dialects coming together in similar proportions and developing at similar times, as well as to parallel developments. I also believe that, in my three-stage approach, as outlined above, I have achieved a probabilistic solution to the problem of randomness and intergenerational transmission.

References

Aitken, A. J., 'Scottish accents and dialects', in Peter Trudgill (ed.), *Language in the British Isles* (Cambridge: Cambridge University Press, 1984), pp. 94–114.

Algeo, John, 'External history', in John Algeo (ed.), *The Cambridge History of the English Language, vol. 6: English in North America* (Cambridge: Cambridge University Press, 2001), pp. 1–58.

Algeo, John (ed.), *The Cambridge History of the English Language, vol. 6: English in North America* (Cambridge: Cambridge University Press, 2001).

Andersen, Henning, 'Preglottalization in English and a North Germanic bifurcation', in D. Restle and D. Zaefferer (eds), *Sounds and Systems: studies in structure and change. A Festschrift for Theo Vennemann* (Berlin: Mouton de Gruyter, 2002), pp. 5–24.

Andrésen, Bjørn, *Preglottalization in English Standard Pronunciation* (Oslo: Norwegian Universities Press, 1968).

Ash, Sherry, 'The United States of America: the land of opportunity', in E. Ronowitz and C. Yallop (eds), *English: one language, different cultures* (London: Cassell, 1999), pp. 197–263.

Asselin, Claire, and Anne McLaughlin, 'Les immigrants en Nouvelle-France au 17e siècle parlaient-ils français?', in Raymond Mougeon and Édouard Beniak (eds), *Les origines du français québécois* (Sainte-Foy: Laval University Press, 1994), pp. 101–30.

Bailey, Richard W., *Nineteenth-Century English* (Ann Arbor: University of Michigan Press, 1996).

— and Manfred Görlach (eds), *English as a World Language* (Ann Arbor: University of Michigan Press, 1982).

Baker, S. J., *The Australian Language* (Sydney: Currawong, 1966).

Barbaud, Philippe, 'Des patois au français: la catastrophe linguistique de la Nouvelle-France', in Raymond Mougeon and Édouard Beniak (eds), *Les origines du français québécois* (Sainte-Foy: Laval University Press, 1994), pp. 79–100.

Bartlett, Christopher, *The Southland Variety of New Zealand English* (Otago University, PhD thesis, 2003).

Batterham, Margaret, 'The apparent merger of the front centring diphthongs – EAR and AIR – in New Zealand', in Allan Bell and Koenraad Kuiper (eds), *New Zealand English* (Amsterdam: Benjamin, 2000), pp. 111–45.

Bauer, Laurie, 'The second great vowel shift?', *Journal of the International Phonetics Association*, 9 (2), 1979, pp. 59–66.

— 'Notes on New Zealand English phonetics and phonology', *English World-Wide*, 7, 1986, pp. 225–58.

— 'The second great vowel shift revisited', *English World-Wide*, 13, 1992, pp. 253–68.

— 'Attempting to trace Scottish influence on New Zealand English', in Edgar W. Schneider (ed.), *Englishes Around the World 2: studies in honour of Manfred Görlach* (Amsterdam: Benjamin, 1997).

— 'The dialectal origins of New Zealand English', in Allan Bell and Koenraad Kuiper (eds), *New Zealand English* (Amsterdam: Benjamin, 2000), pp. 40–52.

— and Winifred Bauer, 'Can we watch regional dialects developing in colonial English?: the case of New Zealand', *English World-Wide*, 23, 2003, pp. 169–93.

Beal, Joan, *English Pronunciation in the Eighteenth Century: Thomas Spence's 'Grand repository of the English language'* (Oxford: Clarendon Press, 1999).

Belich, James, *Making Peoples* (Auckland: Penguin, 1996).

Bell, Allan, 'The phonetics of fish and chips in New Zealand: marking national and ethnic identities', *English World-Wide* (18), 1997, pp. 243–70.

— and Janet Holmes, '/h/-dropping: two sociolinguistic variables in New Zealand English', *Australian Journal of Linguistics* (12), 1992, pp. 223–48.

— and Koenraad Kuiper (eds), *New Zealand English* (Amsterdam: Benjamin, 2000).

Bennett, G., *Wanderings in New South Wales* (London: 1834).

Bernard, J. R., 'On the uniformity of spoken Australian English', *Orbis* (18), 1969, pp. 62–73.

— 'Australian pronunciation', *The Macquarie Dictionary* (Sydney: Macquarie Library, 1981), pp. 18–27.

— 'Quantitative aspects of the sounds of Australian English', in Peter Collins and David Blair (eds), *Australian English* (St Lucia: University of Queensland Press, 1989), pp. 187–204.

Berthele, Raphael, *Sprache in der Klasse: eine dialektologisch-soziolinguistische Untersuchung von Primarschulkindern in multilingualem Umfeld* (Tübingen: Niemeyer, 2000).

— 'Learning a second dialect: a model of idiolectal dissonance', *Multilingua* (21), 2002, pp. 327–44.

Bloomfield, Leonard, *Language* (New York: Holt, 1933).

Bradley, David, '/æ/ and /a:/ in Australian English', in Jenny Cheshire (ed.), *English around the World* (Cambridge: Cambridge University Press, 1991), pp. 227–34.

— 'Regional dialects in Australian English phonology', in Peter Collins and David Blair (eds), *Australian English* (St Lucia: University of Queensland Press, 1989), pp. 260–70.

— and Maya Bradley, 'Melbourne vowels', *University of Melbourne Working Papers in Linguistics* (5), 1979, pp. 64–83.

Branford, William, 'English in South Africa', in Robert Burchfield (ed.), *The Cambridge History of the English Language, vol. 5: English in Britain and overseas – origins and development* (Cambridge: Cambridge University Press, 1994), pp. 182–429.

Britain, David, 'Dialect contact and phonological reallocation: "Canadian Raising" in the English Fens', *Language in Society* (26), 1997, pp. 15–46.

— (forthcoming), 'The British origins of New Zealand English?', in R. Harlow, D. Starks and A. Bell (eds), *The Languages of New Zealand* (Wellington: Victoria University Press).

— and Peter Trudgill, 'Migration, new-dialect formation and sociolinguistic refunctionalisation: reallocation as an outcome of dialect contact', *Transactions of the Philological Society* (97), 1999, pp. 245–56.

Brook, G. L., *English Dialects* (London: Deutsch, 1958).

Bryant, Pauline, 'Regional variation in the Australian English lexicon', in Peter Collins and David Blair (eds), *Australian English* (St Lucia: University of Queensland Press, 1989), pp. 301–14.

Burchfield, Robert (ed.), *The Cambridge History of the English Language, vol. 5: English in Britain and overseas – origins and development* (Cambridge: Cambridge University Press, 1994).

Cappella, J. N., 'Mutual influence in expressive behavior', *Psychological Bulletin* (89), 1981, pp. 101–32.

— 'Behavioral and judged coordination in adult informal social interactions: vocal and kinesic indications', *Journal of Personality and Social Psychology* (72), 1997, pp. 119–31.

Cassidy, Frederick, and Robert Le Page, *Dictionary of Jamaican English*, 2nd edn (Cambridge: Cambridge University Press, 1980).

Chambers, J. K., 'Dialect acquisition', *Language* (68), 1992, pp. 673–705.

— *Sociolinguistic Theory* (Oxford: Blackwell, 1995).

Chaudenson, Robert, 'Français d'Amérique du Nord et créoles français: le français parlé par les immigrants du 17e siècle', in Raymond Mougeon and Édouard Beniak (eds), *Les origines du français québécois* (Sainte-Foy: Laval University Press, 1994), pp. 167–80.

Clark, Ross, 'Pidgin English and Pidgin Maori', in A. Bell and J. Holmes (eds), *New Zealand Ways of Speaking English* (Amsterdam: Benjamin, 1990), pp. 97–114.

Cochrane, G. R., 'Origins and development of the Australian accent', in Peter Collins and David Blair (eds), *Australian English* (St Lucia: University of Queensland Press, 1989), pp. 176–86.

Collins, Peter, and David Blair (eds), *Australian English* (St Lucia: University of Queensland Press, 1989).

Combrink, Johan, 'Afrikaans: its origin and development', in Len Lanham and K. P. Prinsloo (eds), *Language and Communication Studies in South Africa* (Cape Town: Oxford University Press, 1978), pp. 69–95.

Croft, William, *Explaining Language Change: an evolutionary approach* (London: Longman, 2000).

Darot, Mireille, and Christine Pauleau, 'Situation du français en Nouvelle-Calédonie', in D. Robillard and M. Benjamin (eds), *Le français dans l'espace francophone* (Paris: Champion, 1993), pp. 283–301.

de Klerk, Vivian (ed.), *Focus on South Africa* (Amsterdam: Benjamin, 1996).

Dixon, R. M. W., *The Languages of Australia* (Cambridge: Cambridge University Press, 1980).

Dobzhansky, T., 'Biological evolution in island populations', in F. R. Frosberg (ed.), *Man's Place in the Island Ecosystem* (Honolulu: Bishop Museum Press, 1963), pp. 65–74.

Eagleson, Robert, 'English in Australia and New Zealand', in Richard W. Bailey and Manfred Görlach (eds), *English as a World Language* (Ann Arbor: University of Michigan Press, 1982), pp. 415–38.

Ellis, Alexander, *On Early English Pronunciation, vol. 5* (London: Trübner, 1889).

Eustace, S., 'The meaning of the palaeotype in A. J. Ellis's *On Early English Pronunciation*', *Transactions of the Philological Society* (67), 1969, pp. 31–79.

Flikeid, Karin, 'Origines et évolution du français acadien à la lumière de la diversité contemporaine', in Raymond Mougeon and Édouard Beniak (eds), *Les origines du français québécois* (Sainte-Foy: Laval University Press, 1994), pp. 275–326.

Frings, Theodor, *Grundlegung einer Geschichte der deutschen Sprache*, 3rd edn (Halle: Niemeyer, 1957).

Fry, D. B., 'The frequency of occurrence of speech sounds in southern English', *Archives néerlandaises de phonétique experimentale* (10), 1947, pp. 103–6.

Giles, Howard 'Accent mobility: a model and some data', *Anthropological linguistics* (15), 1973, pp. 87–105.

Gimson, A. C., *An Introduction to the Pronunciation of English* (London: Edward Arnold, 1962).

Gordon, Elizabeth, 'New Zealand English pronunciation: an investigation into some early written records', *Te Reo* (26), 1983, pp. 29–42.

— 'The origins of New Zealand speech: the limits of recovering historical information from written records', *English World-Wide* (19), 1998, pp. 61–85.

—, Lyle Campbell, Jen Hay, Margaret Maclagan and Peter Trudgill, *New Zealand English: its origins and evolution* (Cambridge: Cambridge University Press, 2004).

Görlach, Manfred, 'Colonial lag? The alleged conservative character of American English and other "colonial" varieties', *English World-Wide* (8), 1987, pp. 41–60.

Grant, William, *The Pronunciation of English in Scotland* (Cambridge: Cambridge University Press, 1913).

— and James M. Dixon, *Manual of Modern Scots* (Cambridge: Cambridge University Press, 1921).

Hammarström, Göran, *Australian English: its origins and status* (Hamburg: Buske, 1980).

Hancock, Ian, 'The domestic hypothesis, diffusion and componentiality: an account of Atlantic anglophone creole origins', in Pieter Muysken and Norval Smith (eds), *Substrata Versus Universals in Creole Genesis* (Amsterdam: Benjamins, 1986).

Harrington, Jonathan, Felicity Cox and Zoë Evans, 'An acoustic study of broad, general and cultivated Australian English vowels', *Australian Journal of Linguistics*, 1996, pp. 155–84.

Harris, Alice, and Lyle Campbell, *Historical Syntax in Cross-Linguistic Perspective* (Cambridge: Cambridge University Press, 1995).

Harrison, G. A., J. M. Tanner, D. R. Pillbeam and P. T. Baker, *Human Biology: an introduction to human evolution, variation, growth and adaptability* (Oxford: Oxford University Press, 1988).

Hazen, Kirk, *Identity and Ethnicity in the Rural South: a sociolinguistic view through past and present* BE (Durham: Duke University Press, 2000).

Hernandez-Campoy, Juan Manuel, and Peter Trudgill, 'Functional compensation and southern Peninsular Spanish /s/ loss', *Folia Linguistica Historica*, (23), 2003, pp. 31–57.

Herzog, Marvin, *The Yiddish Language in Northern Poland* (The Hague: Mouton, 1965).

Hollyman, K. J., 'Le français en Nouvelle-Calédonie', in A. Valdmann (ed.), *Le français hors de France* (Paris: Champion, 1979), pp. 621–9.

Holmes, Janet, 'Maori and Pakeha English: some New Zealand evidence', *Language in Society* (26), 1997, pp. 65–102.

Horvath, Barbara, *Variation in Australian English: the sociolects of Sydney* (Cambridge: Cambridge University Press, 1985).

— and R. Horvath, 'A geolinguistics of short *a* in Australian English', in Peter Collins and David Blair (eds), *Australian English* (St Lucia: University of Queensland Press, 1989), pp. 341–55.

Hughes, Arthur, and Peter Trudgill, *English Accents and Dialects*, 3rd edn (London: Edward Arnold, 1995).

Hughes, Geoffrey, *A History of English Words* (Oxford: Blackwell, 2000).

Hull, Alexander, 'Des origines du français dans le Nouveau Monde', in Raymond Mougeon and Édouard Beniak (eds), *Les origines du français québécois* (Sainte-Foy: Laval University Press, 1994), pp. 183–98.

Hundt, Marianne, *New Zealand English Grammar – Fact or Fiction?: a corpus-based study in morphosyntactic variation* (Amsterdam: Benjamin, 1998).

Ihalainen, Ossi, 'The dialects of England since 1776', in Robert Burchfield (ed.), *The Cambridge History of the English Language, vol. 5: English in Britain and overseas – origins and development* (Cambridge: Cambridge University Press, 1994), pp. 197–276.

Jakobson, Roman, 'Linguistics and poetics', in *Selected Writings III* (The Hague: Mouton, 1971), pp. 18–51.

Johnston, Paul, 'Old Scots phonology and its regional variation', in Charles Jones (ed.), *The Edinburgh History of the Scots Language* (Edinburgh: Edinburgh University Press, 1997a), pp. 46–111.

— 'Regional variation', in Charles Jones (ed.), *The Edinburgh History of the Scots Language* (Edinburgh: Edinburgh University Press, 1997b), pp. 433–513.

Jones, Charles, *A History of English Phonology* (London: Longman, 1989).

— (ed.), *The Edinburgh History of the Scots Language* (Edinburgh: Edinburgh University Press, 1997).

Juneau, M., *Contribution à l'histoire de la prononciation française au Québec: études des graphies des documents d'archives* (Sainte-Foy: Laval University Press, 1972).

Kallen, Jeff, 'English in Ireland', in Robert Burchfield (ed.), *The Cambridge History of the English Language, vol. 5: English in Britain and overseas – origins and development* (Cambridge: Cambridge University Press, 1994), pp. 148–96.

Keller, Rudi, *On Language Change: the invisible hand in language* (London: Routledge, 1994).

Kent, Ray, and Charles Read, *The Acoustic Analysis of Speech* (San Diego: Whurr, 1992).

Kenyon, J. S., *American Pronunciation* (Ann Arbor: Wahr, 1924).

Kerswill, Paul, 'Babel in Buckinghamshire? Pre-school children acquiring accent features in the new town of Milton Keynes', in Gunnel Melchers and Nils-Lennart Johannesson (eds), *Nonstandard Varieties of Language* (Stockholm: Almqvist and Wiksell, 1994), pp. 64–83.

Kirwin, William, 'Newfoundland English', in John Algeo (ed.), *The Cambridge History of the English Language, vol. 6: English in North America* (Cambridge: Cambridge University Press, 2001), pp. 441–5.

Kurath, Hans, *A Word Geography of the Eastern United States* (Ann Arbor: University of Michigan Press, 1949).

— 'British sources of selected features of American pronunciation: problems and methods', in D. Abercrombie, D. B. Fry, P. A. D. MacCarthy, N. C. Scott and J. L. M. Trim (eds), *In Honour of Daniel Jones: papers contributed on the occasion of his eightieth birthday* (London: Longman, 1964), pp. 146–55.

— *Studies in Area Linguistics* (Bloomington: Indiana University Press, 1972).

— and Raven McDavid, *The Pronunciation of English in the Atlantic States* (Ann Arbor: University of Michigan Press, 1961).

— and Guy Lowman, *The Dialectal Structure of Southern England* (Tuscaloosa: University of Alabama Press, 1970).

Labov, William, 'The social motivation of a sound change', *Word* (19), 1963, pp. 273–309.

— *Sociolinguistic Patterns* (Philadelphia: University of Pennsylvania Press, 1972).

— *Principles of Linguistic Change, vol. 1: internal factors* (Oxford: Blackwell, 1994).

— *Principles of Linguistic Change, vol. 2: social factors* (Oxford: Blackwell, 2001).

Lakoff, Robin, 'Another look at drift', in Robert Stockwell and Ronald Macaulay (eds), *Linguistic Change and Generative Theory* (Bloomington: Indiana University Press, 1972).

Lanham, Len, *The Pronunciation of South African English* (Cape Town: Balkema, 1967).

— 'South African English', in Lanham and Prinsloo (eds), *Language and Communication Studies in South Africa* (Cape Town: Oxford University Press 1978), pp. 138–65.

— 'A history of English in South Africa', in Vivian de Klerk (ed.), *Focus on South Africa* (Amsterdam: Benjamin, 1996), pp. 19–34.

— and Carol Macdonald, *The Standard in South African English and its Social History* (1979).

— and K. P. Prinsloo (eds), *Language and Communication Studies in South Africa* (Cape Town: Oxford University Press, 1978).

Lass, Roger, 'Where do extraterritorial Englishes come from?', in S. Adamson, V. Law, N. Vincent and S. Wright (eds), *Papers from the 5th International Conference on English Historical Linguistics* (Amsterdam: Benjamin, 1990), pp. 245–80.

— *Historical Linguistics and Language Change* (Cambridge: Cambridge University Press, 1997).

— 'A branching *path*: low vowel lengthening and its friends in the emerging standard', in L. Wright (ed.), *The Development of Standard English 1300–1800: theories, descriptions, conflicts* (Cambridge: Cambridge University Press, 2000), pp. 219–29.

— and Susan Wright 'The South African chain-shift: order out of chaos', in R. Eaton, O. Fischer, W. Koopman and F. van der Leek (eds), *Papers from the 4th International Conference on English Historical Linguistics* (Amsterdam: Benjamin, 1985), pp. 137–61.

Le Page, Robert B., and Andrée Tabouret-Keller, *Acts of Identity: creole-based approaches to language and ethnicity* (Cambridge: Cambridge University Press, 1985).

Lightfoot, David, *The Development of Language: acquisition, change and evolution* (Oxford: Blackwell, 1999).

Lipski, John, *Latin American Spanish* (London: Longman, 1994).

Lortie, S., 'Origine des premiers colons canadiens-français', *Actes du Premier Congrès de la langue française au Canada* (Quebec: l'Action Sociale, 1914).

Mæhlum, Brit, *Dialektal Sosialisering: en studie av barn og ungdoms språklige strategier i Longyearbyen på Svalbard* [*Dialectal Socialization: a study of the linguistic strategies of children and young people in Longyearbyen, Svalbard*] (Oslo: Novus, 1992).

— *Mellom Skylla og Kharybdis: forklaringsbegrepet i historisk språkvitenskap* [*Between Scylla and Charybdis: the concept of explanation in historical linguistics*] (Oslo: Novus, 1999).

McClure, J. Derrick, 'English in Scotland', in Robert Burchfield (ed.), *The Cambridge History of the English Language, vol. 5: English in Britain and overseas – origins and development* (Cambridge: Cambridge University Press, 1994), pp. 23–93.

McDavid, Raven, 'Dialect areas of the Atlantic seaboard', in P. Benes (ed.), *American speech: 1600 to the present* (Boston: Boston University Press, 1985), pp. 15–26.

McKinnon, Malcolm (ed.), *New Zealand Historical Atlas* (Auckland: Bateman, 1997).

Maclagan, Margaret, and Elizabeth Gordon 'Out of the AIR and into the EAR: another view of the New Zealand diphthong merger', *Language Variation and Change* (8), 1996, pp. 125–47.

— and Elizabeth Gordon, 'Data for New Zealand social dialectology: the Canterbury Corpus', *New Zealand English Journal* (13), 1999, pp. 50–8.

—, Elizabeth Gordon and Gillian Lewis, 'Women and sound change: conservative and innovative behaviour by the same speakers', *Language Variation and Change* (11), 1999, pp. 19–41.

McLaughlin, J. C., *Aspects of the History of English* (New York: Holt, Reinhart and Winston, 1970).

MacMahon, Michael, 'Thomas Hallam and the study of dialect and educated speech', *Transactions of the Yorkshire Dialect Society* (83), 1983, pp. 119–31.

— 'Phonology', in Suzanne Romaine (ed.), *The Cambridge History of the English Language, vol. 4: 1776–1997* (Cambridge: Cambridge University Press, 1994), pp. 373–535.

McWhorter, John, *The Missing Spanish Creoles: recovering the birth of plantation contact languages* (Berkeley: University of California Press, 2000).

Marckwardt, Albert, *American English* (New York: Oxford University Press, 1958).

Mather, J. Y., and H. H. Speitel (eds), *The Linguistic Atlas of Scotland* (London: Croom Helm, 1975).

Mattoso, Camara Joaquim, *The Portuguese Language* (Chicago: University of Chicago Press, 1972).

Mees, Inger, *Language and Social Class in Cardiff* (University of Leiden, PhD thesis, 1977).

Milroy, James, 'On the sociolinguistic history of H-dropping in English', in M. Davenport, E. Hansen and H.-F. Nielsen (eds), *Current Topics in English Historical Linguistics* (Odense: University of Odense Press, 1983), pp. 37–53.

Mitchell, A. G., *The Story of Australian English: users and environment* (Sydney: Macquarie University Press, 1995).

Moag, Rodney, *Fiji Hindi* (Canberra: Australian National University Press, 1977).

Montgomery, Michael, 'A tale of two Georges: the language of Irish India traders in colonial North America', in Jeffrey Kallen (ed.), *Focus on Ireland* (Amsterdam & Philadelphia: Benjamin, 1998), pp. 227–54.

— 'British and Irish antecedents', in John Algeo (ed.), *The Cambridge History of the English Language, vol. 6: English in North America* (Cambridge: Cambridge University Press, 2001), pp. 86–153.

— and C. A. Melo, 'The phonology of the lost cause', *English World-Wide* (10), 1990, pp. 195–216.

Morin, Yves-Charles, 'Les sources historiques de la prononciation du français du Québec', in R. Mougeon and E. Beniak (eds), *Les origines du français québécois* (Sainte-Foy: Laval University Press, 1994), pp. 199–236.

Mougeon, Raymond, and Édouard Beniak (eds), *Les origines du français québécois* (Sainte-Foy: Laval University Press, 1994).

Mufwene, Salikoko, 'Pidgins, creoles, typology, and markedness', in F. Byrne and T. Huebner (eds), *Development and Structures of Creole Languages: essays in honour of Derek Bickerton* (Amsterdam: Benjamin, 1991), pp. 123–43.

— *The Ecology of Language Evolution* (Cambridge: Cambridge University Press, 2001).

Murray, James, *The Dialect of the Southern Counties of Scotland* (London: Philological Society, 1873).

Nettle, Daniel, *Linguistic Diversity* (Oxford: Oxford University Press, 1999).

Newbrook, Mark, 'Scot or Scouser?: an anomalous informant in outer Merseyside', *English World-Wide* (3), 1982, pp. 77–86.

Nielsen, Hans Frede, *The Continental Backgrounds of English and its Insular Development until 1154* (Odense: Odense University Press, 1998).

Helge Omdal, 'Høyangermål: en ny dialekt', *Språklig Samling* (1), 1977.

Orsman, H. W. (ed.), *The Dictionary of New Zealand English* (Auckland: Oxford University Press, 1997).

Orton, Harold, and Philip Tilling, *The Survey of English Dialects, vol. 3* (Leeds: Arnold, 1969).

— and Martyn Wakelin, *The Survey of English Dialects, vol. 2* (Leeds: Arnold, 1967).

Paddock, Harold, 'Newfoundland dialects of English', in H. Paddock (ed.), *Languages in Newfoundland and Labrador* (St John's: Memorial University Press, 1982), pp. 71–89.

Pauleau, Christine, 'La variation du français en Nouvelle-Calédonie', in Michel Francard and Danièle Latin (eds), *Le régiolisme lexical* (Paris: De Boeck), pp. 203–11.

Payne, Arvilla, 'Factors controlling the acquisition of the Philadelphia dialect by out-of-state children', in W. Labov (ed.), *Locating Language in Time and Space* (New York: Academic Press, 1980).

Penny, Ralph, *Variation and Change in Spanish* (Cambridge: Cambridge University Press, 2000).

Poirier, Claude, 'La langue parlée en Nouvelle-France: vers un convergence des explications', in Raymond Mougeon and Édouard Beniak (eds), *Les origines du français québécois* (Sainte-Foy: Laval University Press, 1994), pp. 237–74.

Quinn, Heidi, 'Variation in New Zealand English syntax and morphology', in Allan Bell and Koenraad Kuiper (eds), *New Zealand English* (Amsterdam: Benjamin, 2000), pp. 173–97.

Rickford, John, 'Social contact and linguistic diffusion: Hiberno-English and New World Black English', *Language* (62.2), 1986, pp. 245–89.

Rivard, A., *Études sur les parlers de France au Canada* (Quebec: Garneau, 1914).

Roach, Peter, *English Phonetics and Phonology* (Cambridge: Cambridge University Press, 1983).

Romaine, Suzanne, 'Contact with other languages', in John Algeo (ed.), *The Cambridge History of the English Language, vol. 6: English in North America* (Cambridge: Cambridge University Press, 2001), pp. 154–83.

Samuels, M. L., *Linguistic Evolution with Special Reference to English* (Cambridge: Cambridge University Press, 1972).

Sankoff, Gillian, *The Social Life of Language* (Philadelphia: University of Pennsylvania Press, 1980).

Sapir, Edward, *Language* (New York: Harcourt Brace, 1921).

Schendl, Herbert, and Nikolaus Ritt, 'Of vowel shifts great, small, long and short', *Language Sciences* (24), 2002, pp. 409–21.

Schmidt, Richard, 'The role of consciousness in second language learning', *Applied Linguistics* (11), 1990, pp. 129–58.

Scholtmeijer, Harrie, 'Taalontwikkeling in een nieuwe polder', *Cultuur-historisch*

Jaarboek voor Flevoland (9), 1999, pp. 71–83.

Schreier, Daniel, *Isolation and Language Change: sociohistorical and contemporary evidence from Tristan da Cunha English* (London: Palgrave Macmillan, 2003).

— and Peter Trudgill (forthcoming), The segmental phonology of Tristan da Cunha English: structure and genesis.

Shorrocks, G., *A Grammar of the Dialect of the Bolton Area, part 1: introduction, phonology* (Frankfurt: Lang, 1998).

Silva Neto, Serafim da, *Intodução ao Estudo da Língua Portuguêsa no Brasil* (Rio de Janeiro: 1950).

Sinclair, Keith, *A History of New Zealand* (Auckland: Penguin, 1959).

Sivertsen, Eva, *Cockney Phonology* (Oslo: Oslo University Press, 1960).

Strang, Barbara, *A History of English* (London: Methuen, 1970).

Sudbury, Andrea, *Dialect Contact and Koinéisation in the Falkland Islands: development of a new southern hemisphere English?* (University of Essex, PhD thesis, 2000).

Thomas, Alan, 'English in Wales', in Robert Burchfield (ed.), *The Cambridge History of the English Language, vol. 5: English in Britain and overseas – origins and development* (Cambridge: Cambridge University Press, 1994), pp. 94–147.

Trudgill, Peter, 'Sex, covert prestige and linguistic change in the urban British English of Norwich', *Language in Society* (1), 1972, pp. 179–95.

— *The Social Differentiation of English in Norwich* (Cambridge: Cambridge University Press, 1974).

— *Accent Dialect and the School* (London: Edward Arnold, 1975).

— 'Linguistic accommodation: sociolinguistic observations on a socio-psychological theory', in C. Masek, R. Hendrick and M. Miller (eds), *Papers from the parasession on language and behaviour. Chicago Linguistic Society 1981.* University of Chicago Press, pp. 218–37. Also in T. Fretheim and L. Hellan (eds), *Papers from the 6th Scandinavian Conference of Linguistics.* Trondheim: Tapir, 1982, pp. 284–97.

— *Dialects in Contact* (Oxford: Blackwell, 1986a).

— 'The role of Irish English in the formation of colonial Englishes', in J. Harris, D. Little and D. Singleton (eds), *Perspectives on the English Language in Ireland* (Dublin: Centre for Language and Communication Studies, Trinity College, 1986b), pp. 3–7.

— 'Norwich revisited: recent changes in an English urban dialect', *English World-Wide* (9), 1988, pp. 33–49.

— 'Two hundred years of dedialectalisation: the East Anglian short vowel system', in M. Thelander (ed.), *Samspel och variation: språkliga studier tillägnade Bengt Nordberg på 60-årsdagen* (Uppsala: Uppsala Universitet, 1997), pp. 471–8.

— 'The chaos before the order: New Zealand English and the second stage of new-dialect formation', in E. H. Jahr (ed.), *Advances in Historical Sociolinguistics* (Berlin: Mouton de Gruyter, 1998), pp. 1–11.

— *The Dialects of England*, 2nd edn (Oxford: Blackwell, 1999).

— *Sociolinguistic Variation and Change* (Edinburgh: Edinburgh University Press, 2002).

— *The Norfolk Dialect* (Cromer: Poppyland Publishing, 2003).

— and T. Foxcroft, 'On the sociolinguistics of vocalic mergers: transfer and approximation in East Anglia', in Peter Trudgill (ed.), *Sociolinguistic Patterns in British English* (London: Edwin Arnold, 1978), pp. 69–79.

—, Elizabeth Gordon and Gillian Lewis, 'New-dialect formation and Southern Hemisphere English: the New Zealand short front vowels', *Journal of Sociolinguistics* (2.1), 1998, pp. 35–51.

— and Jean Hannah *International English: a guide to varieties of Standard English*, 4th edn (London: Edward Arnold, 2002).

—, Daniel Schreier, Daniel Long and Jeffrey P. Williams, 'On the reversibility of mergers: /w/, /v/ and evidence from lesser-known Englishes', *Folia Linguistica Historica* (24), 2004, pp. 211–33.

—, Terrttu Nevalainen and Ilse Wischer, 'Dynamic *have* in North American and British Isles English', *English Language and Linguistics* (6), 2002, pp. 1–15.

Turner, George W., *The English Language in Australia and New Zealand* (London: Longman, 1966).

— 'English in Australia', in Robert Burchfield (ed.), *The Cambridge History of the English Language, vol. 5: English in Britain and overseas – origins and development* (Cambridge: Cambridge University Press, 1994), pp. 277–327.

Wagner, Max, 'Amerikanisch-Spanisch und Vulgärlatein', *Zeitschrift für romanische Philologie* (40), 1920, pp. 286–312, 385–404.

Walker, John, *Critical Pronouncing Dictionary and Expositor of the English Language* (1791).

Wall, Arnold, *New Zealand English: how it should be spoken* (Auckland: Whitcombe and Tombs, 1938).

Ward, A., *Some Problems in the English Orthoepists 1750–1809* (Oxford University, BLitt thesis, 1952).

Watson, Catherine, Jonathan Harrington and Zoë Evans, 'An acoustic comparison between New Zealand and Australian English Vowels', *Australian Journal of Linguistics* (18.2), 1998, pp. 185–207.

Wells, John C., *Accents of English* (three volumes) (Cambridge: Cambridge University Press, 1982).

Wright, Joseph, *The English Dialect Grammar* (Oxford: Frowde, 1905).

Zelinsky, Wilbur, *The Cultural Geography of the United States* (Englewood Cliffs: Prentice Hall, 1973).

Index